What Can I Say? I'm A Product of the 60's

What Can I Say? I'm A Product of the 60's.

A Memoir

By

Anne Stuart Welch

authorHOUSE®

AuthorHouse™
1663 Liberty Drive
Bloomington, IN 47403
www.authorhouse.com
Phone: 1-800-839-8640

First published by AuthorHouse   06/01/2011

ISBN: 978-1-4567-6723-5 (sc)
ISBN: 978-1-4567-6721-1 (dj)
ISBN:978-1-4567-6722-8 (ebk)

Library of Congress Control Number: 2011908023

Printed in the United States of America

Any people depicted in stock imagery provided by Thinkstock are models, and such images are being used for illustrative purposes only.
Certain stock imagery © Thinkstock.

This book is printed on acid-free paper.

Because of the dynamic nature of the Internet, any web addresses or links contained in this book may have changed since publication and may no longer be valid. The views expressed in this work are solely those of the author and do not necessarily reflect the views of the publisher, and the publisher hereby disclaims any responsibility for them.

For Snoopy, Efran and Brokus Welch with love and dedication.

For Powder Puff Welch—Thanks for your continued patience and loyalty.

In Memory of Edgar Harmon and Elaine Shreves Welch

I want to thank my good friends Martha and Tom Perkins, Anne and Irv Parnell, Debbie and Will Anderson, Lynn and Jim Johnson, Joan Rogers, Tommy Miller and Martha Bryant for their help and continued friendship . . . Without the constant badgering of Martha Perkins and Barbara Welch, this book would never have met its deadline.

I especially want to thank Billy Douglas, for without his input and excellent memory, I would never have been able to complete my book.

Prologue

If anyone reading this lived their "Coming of Age" years during the 60s, I hope you enjoy reading my story as much as I did reliving it through each page. I hope you will say to yourself, "Yes, I remember that."

Anyone of this era knows that "I Am a Product of the 60s" is a statement of fact, a way of life, a state of mind and the identity of a generation. The 60s also began the start of the largest sexual and social revolutions of the last century, and the best music ever written. If you, like I, were born in 1946, we also have the distinctive characteristic of being the first of the "Baby Boomer" generation. This year, we represent the largest number of people in this country to turn sixty-five in the same year.

We began as *Baby Boomers*, evolved to *Hippies*, to *Preppies*, to *Yuppies* and now to *Senior Citizens*. How time has flown by!

I also experienced my 60s living in the South, the land of beach music, the Shag, serious high school football, moonshine, Nascar and dramatic racial demonstrations. In the southern part of the United States, as in all areas, we had our share of experimentation with drugs, social demonstrations and "Free Love." (Yes, you kiddies reading this, even us old timers did experience that.) Remember, this was a lifetime before AIDS was even heard about.

Since I was about 35, many of my friends have asked me to write a book. I always said, "I will some day." I was having too much fun and did not have the time. Now, I have the time, and I am sitting at my computer with my beloved grandchild, Powder Puff (four-legged) having a drink and writing as much as I can remember. My life has been interesting, dangerous, and an experience I could have only lived through when I was young.

I have always compared my life with the lyrics of my favorite song by the Tams, "Be Young, Be Foolish, Be Happy."

1

Chapter 1

In the fall of 1960, I entered my first year of high school in a small town in North Carolina called Salisbury. If you are from the South, or know anything about the South, the most important day of the week is Friday. This is the day of The Football Game! On this night, everyone possesses school spirit. We could not wait until classes were over to get ready for the game. In the South, high school stadiums are revered as cathedrals. Memories are made there that will last forever, whether you are the student, the fan, or especially if you are the player. In the South, entire towns show their support on this night.

The dress at the time for the gals was Villager blouses with skirts or Villager dresses, madras blouse, monogrammed jackets and, of course, Weejuns. (You always had to have Weejuns of every different style and color.) Pappagallo shoes were worn for more dressy occasions. For the guys, dress was blue jeans or khakis, madras dress shirts or cotton shirts in the many colors and, of course, Weejuns—never with socks. The tennis shoes were Converse and in all styles and colors. (As my Dad was the authorized dealer for both Weejuns and Converse, my family was happy.) Remember the 60s was the beginning of both the preppie and yuppie generations.

How could I forget the hairdos? The Beehive—the more the tease the better. The Flip—of course we had to roll the bottom with beer cans. Ok, now the guys—mainly crew cuts, but some guy's hair was long enough to part.

In my hometown, after the football game, students went to the largest church for after-the-game-hotdogs and to shag. Of course, most girls had to be home by 11:00PM, the boys whenever they wanted. Isn't it something how time restraints are always placed on the females and not on the males? Some things never change, even now.

The above was repeated after every home game.

As we all know, high school was hell for many people and probably still is.

As usual, I am getting ahead of myself.

When I started first grade, my mother would walk me to school and there I would meet with my best friend, Wills. He and I had been great friends since we were born and had always played together, taken family vacations and referred to each other as cousins. We called each other's parents aunt (In the South, aunt is not pronounced ant.) and uncle. Naturally, when we started to first grade, we ate lunch together, sat beside each other in class and were loved by our teacher. After Christmas came, the worst possible thing that could have happened did. Wills' family had bought a house that was not in our current school district. I cried every day until he left. I will never forget our last meeting in school. We were in the lunchroom sharing our lunch as usual. We hugged, I cried and we said our good byes. Now, I saw Wills every weekend, but it just was not the same.

When I entered the second grade, I was assigned to the most horrible teacher that was ever created. She hated children, and most of all she hated five girls in her class. I was one of the five. No matter how many times our mother's complained, it did not seem to matter.

Evidently, some time from first to second grade, I had begun to gain weight. (A problem I still struggle with to this day.) My teacher made fun of me because I was overweight. She made fat jokes about me in class and weighed me separately so everyone could see. She would state, "Ok, let's see who the fattest is." (Remember, this was the South, and every child was taught to respect their elders, say, "Yes M'AM and No M'AM, Yes Sir and No Sir," and never talk back to their elders.) The teacher, and I use this term loosely, kept on and on. If I made a bad grade, she announced it to the class. But, she was really caught up on the weight issue. If there were any loud noises, she would always ask if I fell. I sprained my ankle once, and had to practically hop around the room. She told me that she would not be surprised if the floor gave in, and since the principal's office was beneath the classroom, I would probably go through the floor and land in his office. Since I spent most of my time there anyway, it would be easier than walking down the stairs to get there. She also told the class that I was retarded. The only reason I know what this meant was that I had a cousin who was retarded, and my parents had explained this term to me.

During this time, my mother was walking me to school every day. After I entered the school, I exited through the back door as was waiting for her when she arrived home. By this time, my parents were spending almost as much time in the principal's office as I.

I prayed for my third grade teacher to be good to me and not make fun of me. There was a shortage of teachers, and by the end of my second grade, the same teacher was asked to teach the same students for the third grade. She asked if everyone wanted to move up to the third grade and have her for a teacher again. The idiot even asked for a show of hands. There were five little girls who did not raise their hands. Can you imagine even asking this question? It did not matter anyway. The entire class was moved up with her. As rebuttal, I imagine, she insisted that I be tested in order to find an idea as to the degree of my retardation. I was not tested until after Christmas of my third grade. Before the results were sent to the school, she had told the rest of the faculty and some students that I was retarded and was waiting until the results came in so I could be moved to a special school.

The big day came, my results were in, and my IQ was reported in the 120 to 125 range. Testing someone in the third grade in the fifties certainly was not the most simple task and hard to determine exact results. It was suggested by the teacher, and backed by the principal, that I was too hyperactive (now ADHD) to handle. My parents were encouraged to send me to a private school. I was ready to leave that school and could not wait. Evidently, my parents felt that I was just too young to leave home—big mistake! They both regretted this decision until the day each died.

As young as I was, and especially after this experience, I must have subconsciously decided that I was never in my life going to take crap off any teacher again. I moved from the category of problem child to uncontrollable child.

This school year was about to end, and I could not wait for the summer to begin. There were about seven girls in the neighborhood with whom I played most days. We were always at each other's homes playing and riding bikes. We had slumber parties regularly and went swimming every day. Always on Sunday, Mother made ice cream. I got to see Wills, his family and everybody else who likes ice cream. Like, who doesn't?

When Wills would come to my house, we would spend our time playing softball, tag, hide and seed, boxing (My Dad had a boxing ring built for us. His main purpose was that I would use some of my energy, but not so destructively,) riding our bikes, and riding our wooden horses in our very own special place, Blue Valley. Wills' sister and my sister also played in Blue Valley, but they were so much older than we were, the four of us never played well with each other.

During the summers, Wills' family and mine always took family vacations together. Most summers we would go to Myrtle Beach, South Carolina, or the surrounding beaches of Crescent, Ocean Drive, Cherry Grove and Windy Hill. Every day at the beach, we would go to the pavilion, ride the roller coaster, eat cotton candy and hot dogs, and then go back to the beach to ride the waves. Sometimes we would eat seafood, go to the House of Wax, pick up shells on the beach and enjoy the warm salty air.

One time Wills went alone to the pavilion, but when he returned, he was really upset. An older boy, whose father owned the pavilion, had bullied him, hit him and knocked him down. Well, I immediately went into my fight mode, stomped to the pavilion, found the culprit and beat the crap out of him. The boy never bothered Wills again.

My job of protector for Wills lasted for many years. I could talk Wills into anything: starting fires, damaging the inside of newly built houses, and anything else I could think of to do. When we were confronted, Wills would always say, "I did it." Wills is still as much of a gentleman today as he was then.

As usual, everything had to come to an end, and my wonderful summer was also coming to an end. On most nights after I returned home from vacation, many of us would play No Bears Are Out Tonight, run after the mosquito truck, catch lightening bugs and watch TV. My dad bought the first TV in our neighborhood. Of course, I took the thing apart. When my mother called to tell him about it, he said, "She has to learn by doing." I also had to prove that I could take something apart and put it back together.

Some of the programs I watched, and were watched by most children in the early to mid 50s, were *Howdy Doody, Winky Dink and You, Paul Winchell and Jerry Mahoney, The Lone Ranger, Roy Rogers (with Dale and Trigger), Hopalong Cassidy, The Mickey Mouse Club, Superman, Captain Kangaroo, George Burns/Gracie Allen, Jack Benny, The Ed Sullivan Show, Amos & Andy, Medic, I Love Lucy, Donna Reed, The Life of Riley, Ernie Novics, Red Skelton, Popeye the Sailor Man* (what a way to introduce spinach to children), *Romper Room, Annie Oakley, My Little Margie, Captain*

Video, Liberace, The Little Rascals, etc. Evidently, the main interview style show was Mike Wallace and Edward R. Murrow. Our parents watched Lawrence Welk. Locally, we watched Fred Kirby and Arthur Smith. (*The Arthur Smith Show* and *The Crackerjack.* I hope I jogged your memories and made you say, "I had forgotten that," or maybe you even said, "She left out a couple."

Every Saturday morning I went to the Victory Theater to see the serials, the original cliffhangers. To name a few: *The Phantom, Radar Men from the Moon, Flash Gordon, Captain Video, Captain America, Lost Planet, Patrol King vs. Sky King, Captain Marvel* and others. I could not wait for the next Saturday to come. I do remember when the polio epidemic came and no one was supposed to go out; therefore, no movies for me until the ban was lifted.

Dad got passes to all of the movie theaters, so I only had to pay for a drink and candy (both 15 cents). My dad would arrange for a cab to pick me up at home and take me to the theater. I would walk the block to dad's store and stay until he took me home.

As I progressed through elementary school, I did what I had to do to get by. I never really excelled at anything but sports. I was always a co-captain and chose the girls first that were always picked last. (To this day, Ginger says that is why she started liking me.) I possessed the ability to make people laugh and was the school clown. To my surprise, I was like a magnet as far as attracting friends, and still am. I was a natural born leader, but did not know where I was going to lead myself, much less others. I still had problems with teachers, but I was never really completely disrespectful while making it clear that I was not going to be run over. I learned later that many students and faculty were actually afraid of me. I find this kind of frightening, but it worked for me.

When I began my first day of junior high (eighth grade), I could not believe it:

Wills was in my homeroom. Although we were older, we still had the same feeling of friendship. We had seen each other through the years, especially during the summers when his family and mine would get together. Now we were back in the same school and in the same grade again! He had become very popular in his elementary school and was quite the jock. With his help, I was elected class president. For the next year the school was ours.

The junior high was the first one in Salisbury, NC. All of the elementary schools within the city were funneled into this one school. Many of the friends I met remain my friends to this day, especially Molly.

Wills and I were getting older, and with our hormones changing, we realized that our relationship had become different. Although we would remain friends forever, there would never be the companionship and special bond as during our childhood.

The summer after this school year, my beach trip included Molly. We had a great time walking and singing on the beach at Ocean Drive. After summer vacation, my sister went away to college, my mother went to work (freedom at last), and I started high school.

I was still mad at my parents for not sending me to a private school. I decided I would take matters into my own hands, and I applied to every military school (I knew I needed the discipline) and prep school within a four state radius. I used my initials and not my full name on each application. Within a couple of months, headmasters and commandants from about fifteen schools traveled to my home town to speak with my father about enrolling me in their school. They were even talking scholarships!

My father must have handled it pretty well because he never really said much to me. He learned by now to expect the unexpected of me. He did have the responsibility of telling the representative of each school that he did not have a son but if they were willing to take on his daughter, that he would be willing to let her go, with or without scholarships. Evidently, they were not willing to do so.

Every Wednesday was golf day for dad and about twenty others. They would meet at our house, and then take about six cars to a particular golf course, usually located out of town. I had about fifteen cars to choose from. Naturally, I decided to joy ride.

I would back out of the driveway, (To this day, I drive better backwards than forwards) and pick up some friends. Usually this would include Ginger, Molly, Liz, Tony and Hank. We would "cruise" for about three hours. Nobody ever asked how I had so many different cars or when I got my license. They, like I, were interested only in getting out of the house and going somewhere. Luckily, nothing serious ever happened.

The next year I turned sixteen at least five months before most of my friends. I continued to be everyone's chauffeur, this time legally. Several of us went out most weekends to Dino's, the drive-in, to blasts, (a party where kids gets together at the house of another person and totally destroy the house) just to drive around or to go to regular parties.

On many Saturday or Sunday afternoons, Ginger and I went to concerts at the coliseum in Charlotte, NC. Popular groups like Peter, Paul and Mary, The Tams, Kingston Trio, The Beach Boys, Brooks Benton, Fats Domino and many others performed. These were fun times.

I went through the rest of high school not wanting to be there, but I did not know where I wanted to be: my mind always in a daze and with little motivation. I always seemed to have more guy friends than girl friends. I guess it was because I told off color jokes, played golf, hunted, smoked, played poker and drank.

Every city kid went to Dino's on Friday and Saturday nights. No county kids allowed, as they had their own hang out in the county called The Pit. Across the street from Dino's was Al's. After taking their dates home, the guys went there, stood around, smoked, drank beer and talked about what base they had gotten to with their dates, or if they had scored a home run. Guys have always exaggerated about their sexual exploits, no matter what their age. I guess not caring what it did to the reputation of the girl was never considered. Sometimes us city girls would be bad and go to The Pit. Guess what? The county boys looked like the city boys.

During high school, I dated seldom. My weight was still a problem, and boys don't often ask fat girls out on dates. I felt a little lonely during prom night, but I got over it. I had been asked to go to the prom, but he was the strangest boy at school, and I had rather stay home than go with him.

On most Sunday nights, the majority of the churches had youth programs. Usually I would pick up Ginger. When I would turn in the opposite direction of the church she would inquire as to where we were going, I did not ever bother to answer. She had known me since Girl Scouts, and should have known that I had no intention of going where I was supposed to go. We would ride around and sometimes just park and talk about our futures. Ginger was a little more naive than I, and somewhat introverted, but was usually up for anything. Maybe I was a bad influence, but she had a wild side that was just waiting to come out.

A sudden stop was put on our Sunday outings when my mother decided to help with the meals at church. I am sure she did this to try and control me and know what I was doing. She should have known by now that this was a lost cause. Since I was given the family car to use to go to the Sunday youth group meetings, I had to start going. I did decide to drive my own car, so Ginger and I could ride together and not have to ride with my mother.

During high school, I ran around with many different people. I never hung with a particular crowd. As a matter of fact, I did not realize there were specific groups (cliques) of girls until I was talking to friends while researching my book. Of course they thought I was crazy; then again, they always thought I was crazy. Molly told me that I was a floater, both in junior high and high school.

During the summers almost everyone went to Myrtle Beach, SC for a week or two. We always had several mothers to supervise, but they were not with us all the time. In the late afternoons and at night, we "dragged" up and down Ocean Boulevard and met guys from everywhere. We went to the pad and shagged.

If you did not want some guy to know your real name, or if you did something you did not want anyone to know, you used Modiene Gunch as your name. Evidently, generations of the 40s and the 50s used the same name.

This name must have been used only in a portion of the South. I asked people from other southern states about Modiene Gunch, and they had never heard of the name. I guess my area was just too original for the other sections of the south. Ginger, who always envisioned herself as a trendsetter, used the name Ophelia Butts.

The guys always had to prove themselves, and some guy from one of the high schools would climb the water tower and paint their schools name or initials on the side. BHS, the initials of my school were painted on the tower numerous times. I asked Wills if he had ever performed this ritual. He said one time he was waiting his turn, when the guy before him was arrested as soon as he hit the ground running. Wills was more interested in a clean record than being known as a "water tower guy."

The sixties were such a great time to spend ones' high school and college years. I have read that the sixties are now considered the last age of innocence. So many world changing and memorable events happened during this decade. The most memorable for me are the following:

- The election of JFK in 1960 (also the first televised presidential debate) was the first presidential election that my generation was really involved in: we could not vote but you would have thought we could.

- The flight of John Glenn, the first human to orbit the Earth (1961)
- The Bay Of Pigs Invasion (1961)
- The Soviets launched the first man in space (1961)
- The Cuban Missile Crisis (1962)
- Marilyn Monroe was found dead (1962)
- The Feminine Mystique was published by Betty Friedman (1963)
- Dr. Martin Luther King, Jr. delivered his "I Have a Dream" speech (1963)
- Cassius Clay, also known as Muhammad Ali, became the Heavyweight Champion of the World (1964)
- The Civil Rights Act of 1964 passed.
- The Los Angeles riots, Malcolm X was assassinated, the New York City blackout and the first combat troops were sent to Vietnam (all in 1965) This particular action was followed by mass draft protests in the U.S. (1966)
- The first Super Bowl, the tragedy of three U.S. astronauts killed during a simulation, the first heart transplant performed by Dr. Christian Bernard, a South African surgeon, all occurred in 1967.
- The My Lai Massacre, Robert Kennedy and Martin Luther King, Jr. were assassinated (1968)
- Charles Manson was arrested, Woodstock and Neil Armstrong, who became the first man to walk on the moon (1969).

This next event deserves its own paragraph. President John F. Kennedy was killed in Dallas, Texas on November 22, 1963. I mourned, as everyone else in the world mourned. How could something like this happen in the USA? Everyone remembers just where he or she was on that day. I was walking down the hall at high school, and was told by one of my best friends what had happened. I was shocked and immediately went to the TV room in the cafeteria. I, like most people, watched TV for the next three days. I had always loved Kennedy, and since we shared the same birthday, May 29th, I felt close to him. When he was elected, the world seemed to come together and Camelot was born. He, Jackie, Caroline and John, Jr. represented the entire world, and we knew that he could handle everything.

I was lucky to see him in person once, and only wish I could have gotten close enough to tell him that with him at the helm, everything looks brighter. I believe that if he had lived, this world would be different. Most of my generation feels the same. I will never forget the conspiracy theories following his death. Even today, if a poll were taken, the results would be split in half.

The main event in the 60s that changed music history, as Frank Sinatra and Elvis had done in the forties and fifties, was the introduction of the first of the "British Invasion." In February of 1964, Ed Sullivan introduced "The Beatles" to the USA. I cried and screamed like all girls my age. They were so cute and had the style of haircut that changed young men's hairstyle from crew cuts to longer hair.

The Beatles were followed by many others: The Animals, Dave Clark Five, Peter and Gordon, The Hollies, The Kinks, The Who, The Zombies, Herman's Hermits, The Rolling Stones and many more.

I feel that the impact of television on the world can only be compared to the impact of the PC many years later. I continued to watch television on a regular basis and really was addicted until I finished high school.

Some popular shows of the mid to late sixties were *Wild, Wild West, The Virginian, Time Tunnel, Tarzan, Marcus Welby, M.D., The Monkees, F Troop, Flying Nun, Mr. Ed, Mission Impossible, Dr. Kildare, Doris Day, Candid Camera, Danny Kay, Wagon Trail, Secret Agent, The Rogues, Ozzie and Harriet, Flipper, Mr. Novac, Burke's Law, Gomer Pyle, Bob Hope Chrysler Theater, The Ed Sullivan Show, Voyage to the Bottom of the Sea, Star Trek, Laugh In, Andy Griffith, Route 66, The Beverly Hillbillies, Perry Mason, 77 Sunset Strip, Batman* sports broadcasts, "the soaps" and game shows were also an important part of this era. I do also have to mention the teen dancing shows of *Hullabloo, American Bandstand* and *Shindig*.

All of the television shows, movies and movie magazines only added to my already vivid imagination and started my desire to travel to Hollywood. I could imagine myself on the arm of Cary Grant. (Even to this day, I prefer older men.)

It was tradition that when my friends turned 18, I would buy them their first legal beer. I remember one time in particular when I took Ginger to buy and drink her first beer ever. She hated the taste, and honestly so did I. We decided to pour the remainder of the six-pack in a cornfield. The next year, we drove by the same field, and the cornfield had more corn than it ever had! We wondered if the farmer ever noticed it.

Graduation was around the corner. As usual, I just wanted to graduate, and I decided I wanted to travel to California. I graduated in 1964, and my class was the last segregated class to graduate from Boyden High School.

Unknown to my parents, I had applied to Pasadena Playhouse and was accepted. I talked Ginger into leaving a couple of weeks after graduation for California. She agreed without hesitation, although she had been accepted at a college in North Carolina. Maybe her adventurous side was beginning to develop. We left one morning without telling anyone and made it about forty miles before my car broke down. Well, there went that trip. Ginger went on to begin her college career, and I thought to myself, "What am I going to do now?"

Following that botched short trip, my mother decided that my graduation present would be a trip to New York for the 1964 World's Fair. My sister and our great family, Mary, traveled with us. We spent about three days at the Fair seeing as many exhibits as possible.

Mary had a friend who lived in the city and she had all of us over for a meal. The friend fixed Quiche Lorraine, and we were served on a Castro convertible coffee table. (This, when lowered, converted into a coffee table). I decided that I had to have one. Our stay in the city was really enjoyable, and we all had a great time experiencing the nightlife, going to famous restaurants, seeing plays and "The Rockettes."

Instead of going home, we decided to travel on to Canada and to Niagara Falls. The trip through the upstate New York area was beautiful, and the scenery and countryside was fantastic. Like so many other people, I had thought of New York as a city of eight million people with only skyscrapers and concrete. As we passed the West Point campus, we stopped to take a tour. Seeing the cadets, in their striking uniforms, was a sight I will never forget. Niagara Falls was wonderful, and the Canadian side is the very best for touring and to experience the best view of the falls.

Our return trip was sad and I began to think again, "What am I going to do now?" My friends were all set and getting ready to start college. I did not know that my mother had already enrolled me in a business college in my hometown. A business college! What in God's name was a business college? I could not type, did not want to learn, and certainly was not going to waste my life typing letters for some man or anybody else. I went for the year, graduated and got a newer car out of the deal. (Remember the 1961 Chryslers with the fins that started with the push button?) I did not realize that the next step was work, but I did know I wanted no part of it. I wanted to travel and live my life with the rich and famous.

I decided I would look for a job in Florida. The majority of my friends were in college, and I really did not have anyone to hang out with. My friend, Liz, had gotten married the year before and had a baby. Her baby was cute, but I was too young to be around babies. My parents said I could go to Florida since Wills was going to college and living in the same town. There was one condition, naturally. I would have to stay at the YWCA. I had no idea what a YWCA was. I had heard of the YMCA, but I was not going to ask any questions. Off I went, my first time in a passenger jet.

After arriving in Jacksonville, Wills met me at the gate and then drove me to the YWCA. Reluctantly, I entered and tried to settle in as best as I could. After about two days, a girl (DJ) was moved into my room late one night. When the dorm person brought her in, it was explained to me that she had moved in on an emergency basis, and that she was Jewish. Why she added this useless bit of information, I do not know.

After the dorm person left, I asked DJ to explain to me why being Jewish seemed to be an issue. DJ explained to me what the initials "YWCA" stood for. She also told me that her stepfather was an old college friend of the present governor of Florida, so the "Y" did not have a choice but to admit her. She also explained that her boyfriend had been abusive to her; therefore, the emergency placement. We hit it off really well. Since we both hated the "Y" and liked our independence, we moved into an apartment about three days later.

She was about a year younger than I, had finished high school at 16, completed a couple of years of college and was still undecided as to what to do next. Now, I knew that we were going to get along fine, as the two of us were undecided about everything. She told me that she had worked for Playboy for years as both a child and teenage model. Evidently she decided to return to modeling. She made her contacts and was scheduled to do some shots in the islands. Of course, I had to go with her.

A private jet was always available to take us to the Bahamas or anywhere else. I had only flown once in a passenger jet, and now I was flying in private jets. Will wonders never cease! This did start my love of airplanes and anything else related to speed.

While she worked, I learned to snorkel, but basically I stayed on the beach all day. On one trip, Gary, the abusive boyfriend, was waiting for her as we departed the plane. Naturally, he and I immediately disliked each other. DJ took him back into her life. To appease DJ, Gary offered to teach me to scuba dive. He was a professional diver, and I agreed to let him teach me. He started my lessons and I entered another world, a world that I continued to embrace for the next forty-six years.

Eventually, DJ completed her work in the islands, and we went back to Florida. I loved Florida, saw the Beatles, rode in a Rolls, ate Beluga caviar (still love it to this day), drank *Dom Pérignon* champagne, went to the best parties and met the best people. DJ knew everyone and introduced me to all of her friends. I attended parties with enough drugs and alcohol to furnish any frat house. I had my first experience, to use the slang for the current time of the sixties, with "sex, drugs and rock and roll." Actually, not the sex part, that was to come later.

Wills and I attended the wrestling matches on most Wednesdays. We saw one wrestler break his opponent's neck, and I was horrified. The next week, I saw the same wrestler in a store buying clothes. Wills was with me and I just pointed. Wills said, "I thought you knew the matches were fake." I never attended another wrestling match.

I was really getting into the sign of the times when I received a call from Dad saying, "Either you come home or the money stops." and "I need you to help in the store." Well, fair is fair. Eight months was really enough time to find some type of job in Florida. I did not tell him that I forgot to look.

DJ moved back in with Gary, and I left for the real world, which I had forgotten all about. I was in for a reality shock when I returned home. When I departed from the plane, I asked myself, "Why didn't I try to find some sort of a job in Florida?"

After a few days of rest, I began working again in my father's business. I had worked in his store since I was fifteen, and really enjoyed it. Since his life was based on fishing, hunting and golfing, his business was not his top priority. I ran the business and was the boss when he was gone, which was frequently. I was born to be in charge, and besides, he and I could not have worked side by side every day. When he was with me, his temperament was as bad as mine, and he had very little patience with me. These traits, were unfortunately, inherited by me from both my mother and father's side of the family.

One day, Dad and I talked about my future and the fact that I needed a college education. My parents had never talked to either my sister or to me about getting married or having children. The one requirement they demanded was that we obtain a college education, because neither wanted us to depend on anyone for anything. As I think back on it, what great advice. Thank God I was never given a guideline as to the number of years I had to complete college.

Chapter 2

How I Turned Four Years
of College into Eleven

Good old mom got an application for college and completed it for me. It was one of those colleges known for accepting a student no matter what their high school grades. This was also a college where the sons, daughters and nieces of congressmen, senators, cabinet members, generals, TV personalities and CEOs of national and international corporations attended. It was a strict Baptist college that did not allow any drinking, smoking, and certainly no fraternizing with the males. Out I headed, knowing the rules were never meant for me.

The college didn't have dorms in the normal definition of two girls to a room and a bath shared by eight or ten other girls. We had suites: four rooms to a suite, two girls to a room, a large living area, a bath with two toilets, two showers and a large garden tub.

I really loved this arrangement and the other seven girls really liked me. I entertained them by lip-synching to my favorite group, The Tams. Sometimes I had to throw in "The Duke of Earl" by Gene Chandler. We would have great fun in our room before lights out. I had a great semester. I made the dean's list and really loved the school. The camaraderie was such a great experience. I feel that everyone should live in a dorm for at least a year.

In the early sixties, having an apartment off campus was not even an option for females. Well-known universities did not have dorms for females and most Ivy League colleges did not allow females in their undergraduate programs at all.

Unfortunately, as I had entered the second semester, everyone else had already chosen roommates for the following year. I had met some nice girls and only one had not chosen her roommate either. Mary had also entered the second semester as I did. We decided to be roommates.

As we began discussing the next year, I began to think that there was something that was not quite right. As she put her hand on mine and expressed her love for me, the light bulb turned on. I was, and still am, a little naïve, but I knew that I was not going to share a room with her. We discussed this, she said she understood, and decided to have the college assign her another roommate.

Unfortunately, I was put in the same position of starting the next school year without a roommate of my choice. I ended up being assigned with someone that was not only a redneck, but also a loser. When I looked around at the other six girls, I realized that they were all rednecks and losers. I guess they were all put in the same room for this reason. Believe me, this combination was quite rare at this college. To paraphrase a statement I understand many mountain people say, "Brothers and sisters must have married each other."

My only salvation was that the next suite contained my good friend, Maggie. Maggie and I had talked about being roommates before the end of the last school year. Maggie's problem was her current roommate, whom I will call Sneaky. Sneaky refused to change roommates. She actually hated Maggie, but was determined to make the situation a hell on earth. Sneaky really was an evil person, but she did not realize with whom she was dealing. Before she realized what had happened, I moved in and she moved out. Evidently, Sneaky never thought of retribution. As a matter of fact, I never saw her on campus again.

The other seven girls in this suite were great and I remained close to them for years and years, especially Saro. Actually, the gay girl, Mary, was in the same suite, and was assigned to room with Maddy, a good friend from my hometown. Mary was nice enough to move into another dorm with her new friends.

To officially make my move possible, it took about two weeks. My mother had to come and meet with the college president. He wanted to speak in person to my mother, and reinforce what a political situation I was entering. As I was sitting in his office with my mother and trying to understand what exactly he was talking about, it came to me. It made no sense. I was a college student, and not interested in who Maggie's family was. After my mother told him that there would be no problem, I was given official permission to share a room with Maggie.

During this last year, (the college was a two year college) I had a great time, I made excellent grades, met new people and was the best liked of anyone of campus. This was not due to my wit and charming personality. I had a new car and I was 21 years old! I am sure that the workers at the ABC store, (liquor store) which was located about 20 miles away, must have thought I was an alcoholic. Sometimes I was just too embarrassed to keep going in the same liquor store. I decided that we would drive to the neighboring state to purchase our liquor.

Remember the garden tub in my dorm room? Well, it was never used as a bathtub. That baby held "PJ"(Purple Jesus, the great combination of grape juice and grain alcohol.) We partied every weekend and we all loved every minute. On most weekends, a group of us would drive to Charlotte and hang out at The Keg. There was always a band and some group singing beach music.

I guess the dorm mothers really did believe that we were studying every night and on weekends. You know, if one does not know what is really happening, one doesn't have to do anything about it.

Maggie, also known as "55", and I had the time of our lives. We would go into the nearest town, and when returning back, we would "moon" the cars when we got to fifty-five miles per hour. We would sneak over the dorm wall just to be the first girls to do it. We would take my car and go anywhere we wanted, and then return to the dorm without getting caught.

Near the end of the semester, we pulled our "leaving campus trick," and were caught by a security guard. He yelled at us to stop, and we ran like rabbits. Most security guards are old anyway and cannot run faster than young girls. He was getting too close for comfort, so I told "55" to break off, and that I would meet her back at the dorm. We split up; I came back to the dorm hearing cheering and clapping, as I actually scaled the ten-foot wall. I fell on the other side, and started running again into the nearest room. "55" was nowhere to be found.

The dorm mothers were alerted that something had happened, and automatically assumed that there were boys somewhere in the girl's dorms. When a room search was conducted, all that was discovered was "55" and I staying in different rooms. That was ok, because girls were always visiting in other rooms. The next morning when I met up with "55", she acted as innocent as I did.

Later on, we learned the security guard had thought he was chasing two boys, (we both had on baseball caps) and had lost these intruders somewhere on campus. The guard did inform me that my car was found near one of the dorms parked on the curb. He must have assumed that the boys had some how taken my car and left it when they were approached by the guards. Remember, no one locked their cars in the sixties. "55" and I laugh about this incident, even to this day.

During this last year of college, many of my good friends from home were getting married or were already married. Wills married Susan, Ginger married Slick, and Molly married Stumpie. By December of the coming year, Saro would marry RK, and "55" would marry Sandy in a full military ceremony with the reception held at the Congressional Club in Washington D.C. Only one of the couples would ever divorce.

Soon my days were over at this two-year school, and I decided to experience the remainder of my college days at a large university. I had heard that the University of Georgia was rated the biggest hell raising college in the country. This information had my name written all over it.

I applied there, and was wait-listed until the second quarter of the following school year. I decided to apply to another college, but within the University of Georgia system. This college was an extension of UGA near Atlanta. I was accepted and placed in student housing about a mile away from campus. My roommate was a real Yankee bitch. She thought she was special and hated the South. Why she ended up in the South, I never did understand. She stayed about 3 months and returned to Yankee land.

I met new friends, and we decided that we would pool our funds and eat our meals together. I was no cook then, nor am I now. I decided I could contribute more by washing the dishes (I bought paper plates) and furnishing the booze. They all agreed, and the six of us, four guys and two girls, became our version of the six musketeers. The other girl, "Moose", who was over six feet tall, became my new roommate. The six of us did most things together. Having four guys around was definitely a plus.

One night "Moose" and I were walking around our apartment complex and saw a line with about forty guys standing in it. Of course, we had to see what was happening. The line progressed slowly as the guys entered and exited one apartment. We were about ten feet away from the apartment when our guy friends came up to us and dragged us out of the line. Naturally "Moose" and I were mad as hell. They informed us that we were in a "train," and they proceeded to explain it us. We laughed all the way home. They did not. Our arrangement was perfect, and we never argued or disagreed about anything. As I had a good friend who owned a bar in Atlanta, I made at least two trips a week for supplies.

With all of my extra curricular activities, I really did not have time to attend classes. I was asked by every sorority to pledge, but I didn't have time for that either. I did manage to attend peace rallies and join several anti-war groups. (About the only subject discussed at this time was the Vietnam War).

I, like so many others my age, began to search for something we could believe in. This was a period of dramatic change. "Give Peace a Chance" was the national slogan of the young, and pot was being used by just about everyone of my generation on a daily basis. I burned my bra (I didn't wear one again for about ten years, and should have changed my name to "sag.") Most people my age were very liberal and involved in some sort of social issues, whether racial, social, sexual or political.

The Establishment, anyone over the age of thirty, was being challenged by the majority of the young. This was the time for protests and civil disobedience. I wasn't a flower child, so to speak, but I did love their slogan, "Make Love, Not War." I did not travel to the Haight-Ashbury section of San Francisco in a VW bus, crammed with at least nine others, with the peace symbol and flowers painted on the side. I enjoy being able to take a shower at least once every day.

I believed that changes needed to be made, and I was concerned with the current issues in my country and the world. I marched with Dr. Martin Luther King, Jr. on several occasions, but when I met Stokely Carmichael during the summer of 1968, I felt entirely out of place.

On a more personal level, I was beginning to wonder if I was ever going to mature, and what was going to become of me. As I was 21, and receiving my own grades, my parents never really knew what I was doing at college. I never stepped my foot on the college campus for anything, much less to attend a class. My grades were nonexistent, or so I thought.

After three quarters of drinking, smoking, marching against the Establishment, partying and doing whatever I wanted, I left this college experience and returned home. This time a four-legged friend accompanied me. She was named Yohann, after my favorite bar in Atlanta.

When I returned to my parents' house, Yohann was married to Happy (another Peekapoo) and they had five beautiful babies. I did not have the heart to get rid of them for at least four months. I gave one to "55" and kept the only male, Mackie. The other three I sold and cried when each left. I realized I could never be a breeder.

Instead of going back to work with my father, I went to work for my uncle, his brother. I wrote copy (commercials) for several of his radio stations and had a talk show. I became somewhat of a celebrity and was given the name "Radio Annie" by my listeners. I had some interesting and controversial guests, and much talk centered on the Vietnam War, riots throughout the country and integration. Personally, I thought the programs were quite good and I certainly received mostly positive calls from listeners.

However, free speech and people expressing their own opinions was not of interest to my uncle. What he really opposed was the music I chose to play. He was stuck in the big band era of Bing Crosby, Frank Sinatra, Perry Como, Tommy Dorsey, etc. Give me The Tams, Four Tops, The Temps, Clarence Carter and all the black groups of the 60s. What music they could sing!

He waited a year to jerk me off the air. There I was enjoying my hour, playing my good music, reviewing commercials I had written, and getting ready to go back to my live program. Suddenly, someone jerks the earphones from around my head, jerks the record from the turntable and tells me, "You are to play my music or none at all." Then the voice added, "Get the hell out of my damn station."

Realizing that my uncle owned the station, he had to be the one speaking. Well, I said to him, "Get the fuck out of my face or it will be the last face you see." I did not realize that the mike was keyed. I walked out, never looking back. How the FCC did not pull his license, I will never know.

I didn't speak to my uncle again for over 20 years, nor did my father ever mention the incident. I thought the "f "word would have sent my father into orbit. Trouble with authority, any authority, has always been a problem for me.

One day Dad said, "You never should work for anyone but yourself. You are too much of a know-it-all and resent all authority. Finish college, like you are supposed to, and start your own business or take over mine.

It is about time you stopped disappointing your mother." He never said much, but when he did, he meant it.

Evidently, this must not have completely sunk in, because I started working for a children's clothing manufacturer. I designed clothes for young boys between the ages of one and ten, and I was a natural. I have always been partial to little boys, and several of my friends, Ginger and Liz had young sons. Every time I designed a suit or whatever, I was able to take a couple and let anyone wear them to promote the item. Tommy and Johnny were supplied in clothes for years. They were sharp for the 70s young man look.

At this time in my life, I was a hot number. Long hair, a slim body at 5'10", wearing mini skirts, (this came about when there was a textile shortage in England) bell-bottom pants and even boots. This felt great for someone who had struggled with weight most of my life. I always had a self-assured look and a "don't mess with me" attitude. This was my normal attitude, whether fat or slim.

It was time for me to fulfill the sex part of the drugs and rock and roll statement. As the sixties had come to an end, I still had not completed college nor had any definite plans for the future. I had experienced many things, but not sex. Well, that was about to end.

I started seeing a young man and we became involved. Sex followed, the condom tore, and I found out six weeks later that I was pregnant. **I actually got pregnant the first time I had intercourse.** Abortions were not legal in my state, but they were legal in New York. I contacted a clinic and booked my airline reservation. Before going to the airport, I had a miscarriage.

This incident did not turn me against sex. It was not the sex I had planned, but I knew it would not stop me from continuing to try again and again. As I had been involved so much with the sexual revolution, it was about time I participated in the fruits of my labor.

I immediately went to a gynecologist, and told the doctor that I wanted "the pill." The times were not as they are now. The doctor asked if my parents knew of this or approved. I explained to him that I was over 21, and I was the only person to approve or disapprove of what I did. With hesitation, he gave me a prescription for "the pill." This "old" doctor probably did not even understand what the 60s were all about, or that my generation was responsible for starting the greatest sexual revolution of any time. (I was so glad that I had taken his car on many Wednesdays.)

I met an older man, Michael, and started a long relationship with him. This relationship lasted off and on for about eight years. I finally realized what sex was all about, and I knew that I was made for it. He was a traveling salesman, but was in my area on a regular basis. After about four months, he asked me to travel with him, and he also had asked me to marry him.

As far as his offer to travel with him, I did not hesitate. I immediately turned in my notice at work. I also said, "Yes." to the marriage proposal. Well, good old Dad decided to hire a private detective to check up on Michael. He found out some interesting information. For one, Michael was married, and for another, he had children. How could this be? **We were getting married! This is when I learned that a man is separated when he leaves his house at any given time or hour of the day.** This really did not deter me, and my father could not stop me from doing what I wanted.

For the first time in my life, I felt I was happy. Of course, Michael promised to divorce his wife as soon as I confronted him with the information from the private detective.

After a couple of months, his wife called me and made the following statement, "If you want him, you can have him." I decided it was time to move on. After all, when the wife calls the girlfriend, and says that even she doesn't want him, where is the mystery, the excitement and the adventure? I felt two things. One, his wife would leave him, and two I would see him in the future. Both ended up being correct.

Don't get me wrong. This was my first time with having a man in love with me and naturally I was devastated. My friend, Maddy, rescued me. She had finished college and had a job on an island off the coast of both Georgia and South Carolina. This was no ordinary island. This was Hilton Head Island, SC. (from now on referred to as HHI) The island to end all islands can also be referred to, as what I like to call, "The Hamptons of the South."

I moved to HHI, and secured a job as an office manager for a construction company. I was the only female with approximately 300 men. Who says, "There is no God?" I was furnished housing on the beach and everything I could want. I was entirely in charge of the job site and all employees. The plant manager was only there occasionally, and he and I became very close. I was in "hog heaven", as we say in the South. The job was great, island living was wonderful, I could scuba, snorkel and sail when I wanted.

Sunday afternoons were always reserved for polo matches. Maddy introduced me to many interesting people. After the matches were over, we went clubbing, shagging, walking on the beach, sailing, etc. Looking over the harbor at HHI is comparable to looking over the harbor at Monte Carlo. Two of the girls Maddy had introduced to me, Faye and Martha, are still two of my closest friends and traveling companions.

I began to think what Dad had said about my obligation to finish college. After all, the rest of my friends had finished college. I decided to try it once more. I completed the application for the college, but this was only a formality. I was a resident of the state where the college was located.

I quit my job, said my goodbyes, looked back over the drawbridge at HHI and cried. Was I doing the right thing, making the right move or screwing up again? Only time would tell. I had bought my own car when I moved to HHI. This car had an 8-Track player. With beach music blaring, I traveled back home to tell my parents of my plans.

They seemed pleased, but I am sure they had the same thoughts as I did. Dad decided to pay off my car and accompany me to help with the driving when I left for Georgia. He was so easy to figure out. He just wanted to play Harbor Town at Hilton Head.

During the time at home, I was in contact with my friend, Faye, from Hilton Head. She called me one day and told me that she was changing jobs and moving to the same city as the college I would be attending. She and I decided to rent an apartment together. Faye told me that after giving her notice, it would take her about a month to move. I already knew when my classes would start and that I would be there several weeks before she would.

In several days, I received a letter from the college, and Dad and I prepared to leave. We packed the car, with much of the room taken up by his golf clubs. After arriving, we found a hotel near the college. After I was settled in the room, I drove him to HHI and dropped him off at Harbor Town. He evidently had already made arrangements, as one of his golfing buddies was waiting outside the clubhouse. We said our goodbyes, and I drove back to the hotel.

For the next couple of weeks, I stayed in the hotel and attended classes. While at the hotel, I noticed that there was a Wendy's next door but it was not open yet. I went over one day, and saw a young girl with an older man walking around, like they owned the place. As I got closer, I recognized the older man as Dave Thomas. Need I say who the young girl was? Mr. Thomas introduced himself, and we proceeded to talk. He invited me to the grand opening the following week. I thanked him and told him that I would be there. Mr. Thomas was given the key to the city and "a good time was had by all."

I had already toured my apartment complex, and was thrilled with the set-up. Aside from the fact that there were two bedrooms and two baths, we ended up being two of four girls living in the complex of 500 young, single men. What odds? Faye arrived within the next two weeks and we settled in.

All the guys in the complex were really nice, had great jobs and liked to party. Every Sunday was Pool Party and Bloody Mary Day. Our back door faced directly across from the laundry room and right in front of the pool. The complex was about ¾ mile from the college, and sometimes I would walk to class.

The good news was all of my classes transferred from the first college that I had attended. Since I was transferring to a quarter college from a semester college, I entered as a junior. The bad news was that I stupidly had named the college "I did but didn't attend" and was placed on academic probation. Oh well, "such is life."

In 1973 women had many choices of majors. This particular college was the only college east of the Mississippi to offer a BS degree in criminal justice. Knowing myself and my personality, my assets and liabilities, I decided this was the major for me. I excelled in every course and was removed from academic probation after the first quarter.

Most of my courses were offered two nights a week for 2 ½ hours. The classes were at night due to the fact that they were composed of about 40% of active law enforcement officers. When I walked into class, I could see the expressions on the seasoned officers faces. They resented the fact that young people coming into class had no practical experience, but would soon have a four-year degree and possibly become their bosses. Needless to say, very few law enforcement personnel ever established anything other than an informal relationship with any of us non-law enforcement personnel.

The classes were small and the professors were very knowledgeable. All had advanced degrees and were attorneys or accountants. Many had actual field experience. We also had some part-time professors who were retired federal law enforcement agents.

The greatest benefit that the college offered were internships. A list was posted outside of the placement office, which we could choose from. Although we only received credit and pay for one internship, I took full advantage of this benefit and signed up for two internships per quarter. I made great contacts and was able to do some positive networking.

Some of my most memorable internships were with the police department's detective division, (like SVU on *Law and Order*, but without the latex gloves) the DA's office and the state tax office.

During my internship with the police department, one of the chief detectives was a black female. We connected mainly because we were in such a minority, and decided that we would stick together. She taught self defense for women at a local gym, and asked if I would be interested in attending. After about a month, we were both teaching. Most of our students were rape victims and victims of physical assault. As time passed and our students came and left, we both felt that we had been of some help. There were times when we would see our student's names on the court docket. This time they were not the victims.

While at the DA's office, I was fortunate enough to hear Melvin Belli argue before the court. In the courtroom, he was like no other attorney I have ever seen. His nickname, "The King of Torts," suited him well, but his other nickname, "Melvin Belllicose," was also pretty accurate, especially if you sat at the opposite table from him as I did. The papers said that the case was not winnable, but Melvin Belli won the case. As the case was heard in closed court, I was fortunate enough "to be in the right place at the right time."

Many interesting people came to the college to speak. One of the most interesting was Mark Lane. At the time, I knew little about him, but I did know that his movie, Executive Action, based on his book by the same name, was about the conspiracy to kill JFK. He told us that he had been living in Europe for about a decade in exile. Evidently, this was due to his opinions and writings. That night several of my classmates and Mr. Lane attended the opening of his movie. The next day, I learned the movie was pulled from theaters all over the country. This book and the movie proved to me, beyond a reasonable doubt, that there was a conspiracy.

A former suitemate of mine, Saro, her husband RK and their son, Ken, were living in the same city and that worked out great for us. As RK never liked me since college, Saro, Ken and I would go to the beach, grill shrimp and get great tans.

I always kept a tan, but when I started using baby oil and iodine, most of my fellow students thought I was Native American. After seeing the red tint to my skin, many asked if I were a combination of both Native American and Jewish. I do have some Jewish and Native American blood. I explained to my classmates that my ancestry is primarily composed of English, Irish and Welsh descent. My classmates seemed disappointed.

Saro and I would play tennis about three times a week, and competed in double tournaments about twice a month. We played great together, and it helped me stay in shape. When not with Saro and Ken, I was usually found studying at the local club where I bartended in exchange for my drinks. (I came out much better than the owner.) I went out most nights when classes were over and continued to date traveling salesmen. Fortunately, I worked it out so that only one would be in town at a time.

Unfortunately, men have always been my downfall. Men are notorious for a couple of things. One, they are not capable of telling the truth. Two, they are incapable of knowing true measurements. (To a man, 4 inches is always 6 inches.) Three, only a man will say that quality is more important than quantity.

I have always started any relationship with a man with only two requests—honesty and sex on a regular basis. If they were not interested in my requests, I would invite them to leave and not waste my time. I am sure that at least 95% of women, who have had personal and sexual relationships with men, will testify that the male species is not capable of telling the complete truth, only the truth he wants us to hear. I decided a long time ago that I would approach dating as a man does—"Love 'um and leave 'um" and do not let your emotions get in the way.

This way of thinking worked for me for a very long time until I met Grant. He is the only man that I have ever been truly in love with. I met him about six months before I was to graduate from college. I finally had met Mr. Right. How can one tell? After meeting so many Mr. Wrongs, you can feel the difference. If there was ever a soul mate for me, Grant was that person.

One day Michael called, as he always did every year within a week of my birthday. How he could keep finding me, I will never know. We never had a sexual relationship again, but we did have a history. I would meet him for drinks, and then we would see whoever was performing that night. Ike and Tina Turner, CCR, Chubby Checker, or Jackie Wilson were usually somewhere in town. As I could never get enough of Tina or Jackie Wilson, I usually chose one or the other. I was glad when Michael left town. Nothing about him really interested me any longer.

Grant would be back in a few days, and he loved to go to concerts. Naturally, I had much rather be with him anyway. He was a much better dancer, and I was in love with him.

Word always got around when a big party was given. One weekend it was a certain actor who loved to make movies in the state where I was living. He rented a house on the water about 10 miles from where I lived. He was known for his parties, his guests, food, etc. I had never seen so many people and such a selection of drugs since Florida. The drugs were flowing like the liquor. These parties lasted for an entire weekend, and some guests stayed longer. The only disadvantage was not meeting the actor. He was never at any of the parties I attended at the home he rented on an annual basis.

During the summer, I would usually go back to my hometown and help run my father's business. During my free time, I learned to fly and loved it. Unfortunately, I have never been able to understand north, south, east and west. I was told by my instructor that I could take off and land better than any student he had ever had. After my ten hours and my solo flight, I would fly every chance I got. Luckily, I had many friends who owned planes, and I would fly with them whenever I could.

Grant would usually come to visit about every weekend during the summer.

Two important events took place that summer. I became a charter member of the Mile High Club, and my Dad got me my very own puppy. He was part German Shepherd and Lab. He was beautiful and all mine. I named him Snoopy, and he went everywhere with me, even in the plane.

This was a good summer. Although I wanted to take Snoopy back to my apartment with me, I know this would be a bad idea. My parents assured me that he would be taken of, but it just wasn't the same. My parents had always had dogs, but I had never had my very own. When I left my parent's house, I felt so sad, but I knew he was better off having a large yard to play in rather than be stuck in an apartment.

When I returned to school, I received a call from my favorite professor. He informed me that the FBI was interested in me, and wanted to talk with me about coming to work for them. He told me that the recruiter wanted to meet with me early the next morning.

I left my apartment, drove to the mall and bought a blue pants suit. The recruiter arrived around 9AM and did not leave until around 12 noon. He was very frank with me and told me that I was the only person that the bureau was interested in at my college.

In 1975, the FBI was in the position of having to meet quotas. The recruiter told me that no white males were to be recruited for at least the next two years. Also, for once in their history, non-lawyers and non-CPAs would be considered for employment, and criminal justice majors were to be chosen first. Black females were first on the recruitment list, black males followed and then white females. There was also the requirement of two years of administrative experience, but I felt I met this requirement.

I began training for the physical tests, and believe me, this was no easy task. One physical requirement was that I had to be able to run 2½ miles in seventeen minutes or less. I went into training immediately. I mapped out a route and began training for this run and all the other physical requirements. I would start training in the morning and continue through the afternoon. As long as it took the recruiter to get back in touch with me was the deadline for my run.

When the big day came, I left for the school track. Faye, (whom I had nicknamed Chandelier) had taken time off from work. I ran the 2½ miles in less than the required time, but I felt that I was going into cardiac arrest. I ran by the instructors and did not slow down until I arrived at my apartment. I then continued through the apartment, jumped over the furniture, and headed outside toward the pool. I jumped in the pool, clothes and all. Everybody in the apartment complex was cheering me on and had a drink waiting for me. I refused the drink, but began drinking bottles and bottles of water.

The next requirement was on the range. I had been a hunter all my life, had targets in my backyard and had become an excellent shot. The psychological testing was discussed, and I decided that I was as ready as I would ever be.

The background investigation was to be the most thorough. When I asked what areas would be involved, I was told it would cover all the cities I had lived in. I prayed no one in Jacksonville who knew me was still around, and hoped the ones in HHI would have a lapse of memory. After I thought about it, I decided that the FBI needed some new blood and I should not be concerned about the background investigation. After all, my experiences were no different than most who "came of age" during the 60's.

After several conversations and contacts with the Washington office, it was decided that did not meet their basic requirement for the two years of administrative experience. My past working experiences did not qualify as administrative. The contact agent informed me that after I graduated and was settled in a job, I would be assigned a new contact agent. I guess their quota was still fresh in their minds.

Grant and I talked about my possibilities. He was excited, but asked if he could reserve his comments until I decided which job I would actually accept, before we made any definite plans regarding our future. He reminded me that I had several months to decide and to consider my options. After all, I had to complete college and continue with my exercise routine.

Remember, in this era, potential employers actually came to the college campus, set up booths, interviewed students and hired them on the spot. It is a shame that this practice does not apply today.

All of the state agencies that contacted me did not require the two years administrative experience. All the federal agencies required the same as the FBI. I had no choice. I would have to work for a state agency for two years. Which state or which agency, I had no idea. I continued to receive job offers from states over most of the country. I knew two things for sure. I would never wear a uniform and never drive a marked car.

My mother and father were ecstatic and called every day to see what my decision would be. I told them that I would have to discuss it with Snoopy. Time flew by and graduation was around the corner. As I was older than most students, I did not walk nor attend graduation. Every potential employer had my current personal contact information: therefore, I continued to share the apartment with Chandelier.

About a month after graduation, I received a call offering me a position in the state where my parents lived. This agency enforced the alcohol, drug, prostitution and gambling laws for the state. If I accepted, I would be the first female law enforcement officer hired in the State of North Carolina. I inquired if I would have to wear a uniform or drive a marked car. "No," was the answer. "Yes, I will accept the position," was mine.

I was to report to the state capitol building in fifteen days. The waiting was over and my decision was made. I called to inform my parents, Grant and Chandelier of the news. That night, Grant, Chandelier, her date and I celebrated.

After spending the next week packing and loading a U-Haul truck, which included my car, I headed back from whence I came.

Since dancing and music have always been an important part of my life, I feel that I need to devote some space in my book about it. This seems to be a good place.

The Shag is my favorite way to dance, and is similar to the old type of swing dancing. The phenomenon of shag dancing began on the east coast at Myrtle Beach, South Carolina. It is the state dance of both North and South Carolina.

Every year since 1980, SOS (Society of Stranders) has hosted weeklong events in Myrtle Beach. Anyone can shag until they drop during the competitions. Anyone attending will witness some of the finest dancing and dance moves anywhere in the world. Most information states that shag dancing runs from Virginia Beach, VA to Savannah, GA, where it is almost revered as a religion.

Of course, you must shag to real beach music: The Tams, The Embers, The Clovers, the Cavaliers (Southern groups) and Jerry Butler. (Almost Southern)

You can shag or just enjoy the music of Curtis Mayfield, Tina and Ike, General Johnson, The Platters, Jackie Wilson, Bill Deal, Bill Haley, The Coasters, Clifford Curry, The Drifters, Clyde McPhatter, Maurice Williams, B.B. King, Fats Domino, The Spinners, Marvin Gaye, Wilson Pickett, Clarence Carter, The Showmen, Chuck Berry, (the real father of rock and roll) the many sounds of Motown, Elvis and the British invasion groups. I am sure there are others, but you get the idea.

I don't want people to think that shaggers do not recognize other types of dancing. The Twist, The Jitterbug, The Jerk, The Dirty Dog, The Bump, The Stomp, The Mashed Potato and The Hand Jive all have great moves and are fun dances.

Chapter 3

Finally A Career

On the morning I was to be sworn in as an officer for the Alcohol Beverage Control Commission, I traveled alone to the state capital. My parents were driven by an assigned driver from the Secretary of the ABC Commissioner's Office.

The Secretary of State swore me in. In attendance was the Governor, The Secretary of the ABC Commission, his assistant, the local congressman and senator from my parent's district, and my proud parents. I noticed that there were cameras present, but I did not envision that the ceremony was being taped.

After the ceremony and reception, I was given an ID with a badge, the standard issue Smith and Weston 38, a box of 38 specials, the name of my new supervisor, and the address of the office where I was to report to work the next day.

As I was driving home down I85, so many thoughts were going through my head. I decided to take the next exit, pull over and think about what had just happened to me. My temper had always been a problem, and I had never thought about controlling it. Well, the time had come and the day was here that I could legally do things I had previously just thought of doing. This "Pistol Toting Mama" glanced over at the 38 and came to the realization that now things were different, and I had to change my way of thinking. Slowly I headed back to the interstate and proceeded south.

The next morning, I drove to my assigned office in Charlotte and parked. As is my pattern, I arrived early and waited for about forty-five minutes. Soon several unmarked cars arrived. I looked at each guy as they entered the office, (now my office) and decided without a doubt, that the man who was 6'5" had to be my supervisor.

When I entered the office, all heads turned and looked in my direction. Each seemed to recognize me and started shaking their heads. I looked over to the first office on my left and out walked the lanky 6'5" man with a Colt 45 attached to his belt. He looked straight down at me and said something to the effect, "Do you realize that your effectiveness is shot, and I don't know how I can use you now. By the way, you look better in person than on national TV. Come into my office and close the door behind you." I followed his instructions even though I was a little hesitant to close the door. Once inside his office, I sat down, crossed by leg and looked straight at him. He looked straight back and said, "I have heard all about you and like what I hear. You can handle yourself around every man in and outside of this office. Outside of this office is where you need to be careful."

He asked if I realized that one of the major reasons I was hired was for undercover work. He then asked if I watched my swearing in ceremony and my interview with the Secretary of State on television the night before. He continued to tell me that the newscaster announced (using my full name) that I would be working undercover out of the Charlotte office. He also informed me that he had gotten calls all through the night, not only from the men within his office, but from about every lounge and topless club owner in a four county area. Evidently, he had been sworn to secrecy regarding me, the first female who had ever been hired in North Carolina as a state ABC officer.

I just stared at him and tried to let everything he had said sink in. As I have never been the type of person to be without words or a comeback, I felt a little uncomfortable. I guess there is a first time for everyone.

I finally told him that I had not seen the broadcast, nor did I realize that it was being filmed for TV. (What really concerned me was the fact that my full name was broadcast over the airways.)

I looked at him and said; "I think I'll need a bigger gun and yours will suit me fine."

He laughed so hard that he actually turned red. Then he smiled with the warmest smile I had ever seen and said, "I love a good sense of humor. Welcome to the best office in the state." I knew from that moment that JB and I would have a great working relationship and friendship. However, he never offered me his gun.

He ushered me out of his office and proceeded to introduce me to my fellow agents. The rest of the day went fine.

The first issue at hand was to find an apartment, so I asked the guys in the office if they knew of any. I got the blankest stares. What a stupid question to ask married guys. I decided to call around and found an apartment complex that accepted pets. They were running a special: all utilities included with a two bedroom, two bath end unit townhouse. I asked if they would throw in a washer and dryer, and I was told they would. I signed a lease and prepared to move in.

My furniture, what there was of it, was still in the U-Haul at the end of my parent's driveway. All I had to do was get Dad to drive it to the new apartment and have someone move the furniture in. Most of my co-workers volunteered in exchange for beer and pizza.

As the guys were unpacking, I ordered the pizza and beer and left to buy a component system. I got the biggest speakers I could find, and the turntable played both 33 1/3 and 45 records. I headed home so the guys could wire the speakers all over the apartment. I had to have my music, and for the rest of the night, beach music could be heard everywhere with a little Steppenwolf and Fraternity of Man thrown in.

Since I was the new kid on the block at work, I was given an older car. It was ok, but would have been better if the blue light would work without having to throw it about two times against the dash. The siren never worked. How was I going to catch the bad guys?

Work was great, and I spent most of my time studying and memorizing the statutes. Usually, everybody was in the office on Mondays. If I would ask for a paper clip or anything, seven eager guys would rush over to my desk with whatever I asked for. I loved it! I tried not to take advantage or play the sex card, but sometimes I just could not resist it.

As I was new on the job, JB would drive me whenever I went into the field. He would take me around the area assigned to me, and introduce me to everyone he felt I needed to know: police chiefs, the sheriffs of neighboring counties and everyone else he felt I needed to meet. The mayor of Charlotte was his best buddy, so we had lunch with him. I was given the best area, which was the safest in Mecklenburg County, and I told JB that I did not want special consideration. He never answered or made a comment.

One day while we were out, I asked him to take me to the local police supply. I needed some supplies. I never carried a pocketbook; therefore, I needed a shoulder holster and lighter handcuffs, as my heavy state issued ones kept falling off in the toilet. I always wore pants suits but never could find ones with belt loops. Women's clothes just were not made for female cops.

He turned around and headed for the police supply. I bought a shoulder holster and ordered stainless steel handcuffs with my initials on them. When you are in law enforcement, you have to buy everything associated with it. You may never use all that you buy, (How many guns can you wear at one time?) but you have to buy them.

The regular weekend work schedule consisted of four of us split into pairs. As I was the only female, I was drug to every sleazy topless joint and club in the county. I would be sitting alone and wishing I had a book to read, when one of the topless dancers would come over to me and shake her boobs in my face. I knew my partner, JL, had put her up to it because he was off to the side doubled over laughing. When we finally left, **I reminded him what payback is.**

The four of us would usually meet for supper on the nights we worked. We switched partners once a month in order for each of the guys to get used to working with me. All but one was married, and only one of the guys, for some stupid reason, never told his wife that he had a female partner. This particular guy really was a wild card and no other agent really enjoyed working with him. It took a while for everyone to trust me and realize that I would have their backs when the situation arose.

On the weekend I was off, Grant and Snoopy would visit. I was working such odd hours, that Snoopy remained with my parents and their two dogs. He was growing, but was still my baby. Grant had moved about ninety miles from me, and we started talking about our future again. His ex-wife was such a dependent female, and during our time together, she would call to ask the most stupid questions: "How do I change a light bulb? What do I do when the car runs out of gas?" and many too ridiculous to mention. I knew that Grant missed his children, and I am sure that they missed him. He and I really loved each other, but I did not know whether I could put up with the ex-wife and children.

I also had to think about my career. My career was just as important as his, and it would be hard to have the job I had and be married. We both had much to think about.

Time passed and I was getting into the swing of things, calling on the businesses in my area, continuing to memorize the general alcohol statutes and adjusting to my new life. I also had been meeting with my newly assigned contact agent with the FBI since moving to Charlotte.

One night JB called me at home and asked me to meet him early in the morning for coffee, and not to plan to go into the office. I met him at the designated place, got into his car and he headed out of town. We talked normally for about an hour, and then he turned off the main highway onto a dirt road.

At the end of the road, three unmarked cars were parked. He got out and I followed his lead. At the same time we got out of his car, six men exited their cars. I had seen enough "Feds" to recognize that these were Feds but not FBI. The looked at me and back at each other and agreed I did not look like the same girl as the one interviewed on TV.

JB made the introductions, and we agreed to assist with an undercover sting operation that would cover a multi-state area. We left, and I knew without saying, that I was never to mention this meeting to anyone.

The next day I reported to work, JB informed me that I was ready to begin working undercover in Charlotte and statewide. Ok, I could do this. I had been going to clubs and bars since I was nineteen. Surely illegal clubs could not be that different.

As undercover work usually requires working nights and weekends, I realized that my social live would come to a halt. I had to remind myself that I had chosen this career, and I had to accept the terms.

JB gave me directions to the liquor houses and the clubs. I began locally, but also ended up in areas that I doubt God even know of. I have always had a terrible sense of direction, and I would drive hours and waste so much time attempting to find the places. There were many occasions I would speed down the highways in order for a patrolman to stop me, so I could obtain directions. In 1975, no GPS or cell phones existed.

Once a competing legal club owner volunteer to go with me. Doug was about as reliable as a dead battery. I believe he just wanted to go for the gambling, the women and the liquor. Doug drove his car, but I took the keys away from him before we entered the club. I knew that JB was somewhere close, watching us through his binoculars.

When we entered the honky-tonk, Doug immediately disappeared. I was there to buy my liquor and leave. Since Doug was nowhere to be found, I proceeded to play pinball. About thirty minutes later, the owner came up to me, snatched my bottle of liquor away, slammed my money in front of me and said, "I don't sell liquor to ABC officers." He also mentioned my full name.

I quickly turned around, entered the only other room, and found Doug with his pants around his ankles and drunk as hell. I told him to get his damn pants on, practically pushed his "flavor of the night" against the wall, literally dragged him outside and threw him in the car. I spun out of the drive throwing gravel everywhere as the back window exploded. I really think the gravel and the erratic movement of the car kept us alive. As I hit the black top, I could hear sirens in the distance. I drove about two miles and almost ran into two highway patrol cars and JB.

JB was the kind of person who always maintained complete control, but not that night. I almost felt sorry for Doug, but not too sorry. Doug never came with me again anywhere. He sold two of his most profitable topless clubs and joined the Merchant Marines. People we were dealing with don't "play," especially when one of their own turns informant.

Because of this incident, I was burned in that county. It was decided I would not enter this county again for at least six months. That was fine with me. I was a little tired of trying to locate places I could not find and of rednecks spitting chewing tobacco at my feet.

The next night I began working closer to home. Actually, the illegal clubs were as nice as any legal club I had ever visited. All had live bands, nice dance floors and strong drinks. I need to correct myself: the main difference was that all of these patrons carried guns.

I guess everyone has his or her own system when going undercover. My system is to order straight vodka, take the drink to the bathroom, pour it into an evidence bottle, go to my car, label it and hide the evidence in my car. I would then reenter the club and stay as long as I wanted. JB never discussed a time limit for me to be in a club.

On this particular night, I was enjoying myself when I looked around and noticed a very young clean-cut guy with short hair enter the club. He looked around and then left. He could not have been any more conspicuous if he had worn his trooper uniform, and I was not the only person who noticed him.

After finishing my conversation with the bartender, I decided to go to the bathroom in order to exit the back door, which I located while snooping around earlier. I exited the club, got into my car and slowly drove down the mountain. After about five miles, I noticed headlights about sixty feet behind me. I pulled off the main highway onto a dirt road, and then drove about a mile with my lights turned off and pulled over to the side of the road. I quickly exited the car and stepped behind a tree.

I waited for the other car to come up the road and noticed that the driver blinked his lights and stopped his car. JB and the young man, whom I had seen in the club, got out of the car. I came from around the tree and JB had that worried but relieved look on his face. He asked my why I had stayed in the club so long and told me that we was too old for this mess. I asked him if he followed the other agents and timed how long they stayed in a club. He mouthed something about that being different.

I decided that the young trooper did not need to listen to any more, so I suggested that we go home and talk later. That was ok with JB but I could tell this was not ok with him. He did get back in the car, and he and the trooper drove off.

I called JB the following day, and asked to meet with him after he returned from church and finished lunch. He came to my apartment, and I tried to explain to him that I appreciated him caring about me, and not wanting me to be injured or killed, but I need to be treated like the male agents. I chose this profession and I realized the dangers. I asked him to remember when he was young and felt invincible. I do not believe any of what I told him ever sunk in.

JB was probably about twenty to twenty-five years older than I, and his older daughter was about four years younger than I. I also understood that his generation and his ideas regarding women in general, and in the workplace, were completely foreign to me and vice versa. I also knew that the powers that be in Raleigh would blame him if I were seriously hurt or killed. I respected JB, and for me to respect anyone was quite an achievement.

Something had to give with the total protection detail. The other agents in the office already thought JB favored me and were a little jealous. He told me that he would back off. I do not believe he ever followed me again. If so, he stayed well hidden.

Due to my hectic and erratic work schedule, Grant and I agreed to wait awhile before making any definite decisions regarding our future together. I really felt that the separation from his children and my feelings towards children in general, was too much of a strain on him. I am sure we both saw the writing on the wall.

It seemed that my apartment became the hang out for all the guys at the office and many from the local SBI (State Bureau of Investigation) office. Guys were at my apartment about every night. I guess anything was a release from their wives and children. As I had many more interests than they did, I gave a key to the one agent I trusted most not to abuse the situation.

It wasn't long before I was introduced to a nice older man. He had been a senator and lived in a neighboring state. He was fun to be with, but a second rate sexual partner. He had a horse farm, and many times we would go riding and barrel jumping. I had more fun with him jumping barrels than in bed with him. We mutually decided that we would remain friends and date other people. Thank God he was agreeable, and told me that his plane and my favorite horse would always be available to me. Sometimes when he had a political function to attend, I would be his guest. We remained friends for years and had much more fun as friends.

JB contacted me one night, and told me to drop everything I was doing because he has a special assignment for me. This assignment came directly from the state office and required that I work with a partner. My current partner was chosen because he also played golf. As we had worked as partners many times, I thought this assignment would be fun.

When I was told where we were going, I was not happy and was very hesitant. We were going to The Carolina in Pinehurst, North Carolina. This was probably the most prestigious hotel I had ever seen. From the distance, it looked like a picture of the plantations in the South 150 years ago.

Most of the golf courses in Pinehurst, with the exception of Augusta National, are the most beautiful and well-kept course in the country, if not the world. What I could not understand was why we were being sent there. Evidently, somebody had reported the clubs and hotels for selling alcohol to non-members. I guess we could not discriminate because everybody is equal in the eyes of the law. Does anybody reading this believe this? If so, I have some land in Florida for sale!

I knew that my father and uncle played the courses at Pinehurst at least once a year and were well known there. I did not want to run into either one of them. I called my father and found out that neither he nor his brother planned to go to Pinehurst anytime soon.

My partner Sam and I prepared to leave in a new luxury car with out of state plates. We were going as a married couple, had memorized and even rehearsed our cover story. Off we went. We stayed about four miles from the main club. As we were only to go to the clubs at night, we decided to play golf during the day.

When we arrived at the course, we met a lovely couple, immediately formed a friendship and decided to play a round of golf. Before we could even tell our lies, we found out that they were staying at the same hotel we were and just two doors down. Of course, Sam and I were staying in separate rooms; therefore, the "married couple" lie had to be revised and quickly.

Ad-lib, or maybe even lying, seemed to come easier for him than me. After we finished the front nine, the couple asked if we wanted to have drinks with them that night. I suggested The Carolina, and we agreed to meet them around ten that night.

Sam and I went to the dining room about eight. We had no trouble getting in, ate our supper and ordered our first round of drinks. Our friends met us about the time we ordered our second round. We danced, drank and talked until after midnight. The bill for the meal was separate from the bar bill. Sam used his credit card with his new name, and I realized what came next.

The bar required payment with a membership number. This time I improvised, and gave the waiter a number. He disappeared to check the number and make a telephone call. When he returned he thanked us, and the four of us left.

While we were waiting for the cars, the guys agreed to meet on the golf course the next day. I decided I wanted to shop. I just could not keep telling lies to these nice people!

As soon as we got in the car, Sam could not wait to ask me what number I had used for the drinks. I just looked at him and told him it was not any of his business. I never told him whose number it was.

We went to a different club for the next three nights. One club we entered as a couple, and the other two we entered separately and sat separately. Sam was refused, but one club sold to me.

Although we were planning on staying for two weeks, I was ready to leave. We had completed our assignment. I called the state office, spoke with the Secretary and reported what had happened and not happened. We were instructed to leave. As Sam was mad at me for leaving so soon, I drove back. As the driver controls the radio, his country music station was changed to beach music. Sam did not speak during our trip back.

The following weekends were uneventful and work went on as usual. I changed partners a couple of times. One weekend, I was assigned a guy in the office I never really liked. He was a "kiss ass" if there ever was one. He thought he knew everything about everything because he had a college education.

I never understood this way of thinking. A college education does not and never will make a person smarter than someone who does not have a degree. The main advantage is when a promotion becomes available an employer may choose the candidate with the degree over the one without. College boy (CB) also felt a little threatened by my relationship with JB. He was always the "fair-haired" boy, but this situation was beginning to change and quickly.

One night about 2 AM, CB and I were partners for the weekend. He decided to drive to the most dangerous and red neck area in the county. He called the other two agents and asked them to meet us. We waited for about fifteen minutes until they drove up, and I could tell that JL and Mark were as irritated as I was. Our shift ended at 2 AM.

CB wanted to check on some establishments to see if he could cite someone for "after hours sales." (State laws dictated that no liquor could be sold after 1 AM except during daylight savings time) CB knew just the place he wanted to check. He and I walked up to the door of the club, which looked no larger than a master bedroom. He tried to open the locked door and then knocked on the door. In a drunken voice, he demanded entrance.

I noticed that the smart college boy was standing right in front of the door. At the same time I told him to get away from the front of the door before he got shot, the top panel of the door shattered. He had just moved in time and turned a shade lighter. It immediately reminded me of the song by the Procol Harum, "A Whiter Shade of Pale."

The other two agents immediately called in a Code 32 (officer in trouble) and took cover. CB jumped off the side of the porch, (away from the door) and I jumped down the steps on the other side. CB yelled at the person inside and demanded that he come outside. In about a minute, an old, slender and unhealthy looking man came out, gun to his side, dropped his gun and put his hands behind his head. I guess being arrested was a regular occurrence for him. He was immediately subdued, and as I was known as the handcuff expert, I did my thing.

Even though in my short time as a law enforcement agent, I had had shots fired at me and guns pointed at me and the adrenaline rush never diminishes. The four of us were on such a high that we never noticed the sirens or the presence of any other people but us.

As we were coming off our high we turned around saw about fifteen other law enforcement personnel. It makes no difference what agency you are working for, or what jealousy may occur between agencies, a call for help brings all fellow officers. The brotherhood among police officers is the strongest tie one could ever experience.

CB and I transported the prisoner to the county jail. On the way, the prisoner made statements to the effect that he had been closed and was not doing anything wrong. He said we had tricked him into thinking someone was going to rob him, and he was just protecting himself. I was glad this was not "my arrest."

We arrived at the jail, and I insisted that CB do all the honors and receive all the credit. I would not have touched this case with a ten-foot pole.

As I was waiting for Mr. College Boy to finish his reports, an officer came up and told me that I had a phone call. It was almost 5 AM, and I could not imagine who would be calling me. When I answered the phone, it was none other than JB. He wanted to know what the hell happened but was glad to hear that no one was hurt. I wondered to myself how in the hell could JB find out what had happened only a couple of hours ago. I had heard that JB had contacts everywhere and that it was almost impossible to do anything without him finding out.

He proceeded to tell me that the newspaper and the local television stations wanted to confirm, "A shot was fired at the first female hired as an ABC officer." I informed him that a shot was fired at all of us, and quickly explained the story. I told him he could come by later, but I really needed to tell my parents personally about the story. I did not want them to hear the news on television, read the paper or be contacted by the media. He said he understood and asked me to call him when I returned. As I was about to leave the police department, I remembered I did not have a car. I asked the first uniformed officer I saw if he would take me home in order to get my car. I left college boy a message that I was leaving and to take his time in completing his paperwork.

I drove to my parent's house and explained the situation. From my father's comments and body language, I realized that my father finally considered me an adult and an equal, for the first time in my life.

When I returned from my parents, I called JB. He came by and showed me the edition of the paper that mentioned the shooting. While I was skimming over the article, I realized that the paper had misspelled my name. We both laughed about that and I know that my celebrity had faded, thank God. I began telling JB what had happened, that I felt as though CB had entrapped the guy he arrested. He appreciated my candor but did not make any comment as to my report of the incident. JB was the kind of man who always thought things out before taking any action.

When I arrived at the office the next day, CB was in with JB. The other agents wanted me to tell them what had happened. I decided that I would wait for CB in order for both of us to tell them together. Before this could happen, a deputy came into the office to serve papers (a lawsuit) on the arresting officer. Evidently, papers were also on the way to Raleigh. Our most senior agent knocked on JB's door to tell him, and CB the news. The rest of us decided to go for coffee.

As it turned out, the guy who was arrested died before the case involving the lawsuit could be heard. He had cancer. No wonder he looked so weak and pale. CB asked me later what I would have said in court. I told him that I would have answered truthfully. I further explained to him, "When I place my hand and swear on the Bible, I would not go to hell for him or anyone else." Not because of my statements or anything in particular, CB and I seldom worked as partners again. Our agency, in general, was in the process of major changes.

About a month later, the name of our agency was changed and our job titles were also. Our new ID and badge were really professional looking. We were now known as Alcohol Law Enforcement Agents.

Another big change was mandated by the legislature. The SBI was given the official authority for enforcing the drug laws for the state. This was better. As far as I knew we had never officially been trained in drug enforcement. We were only given authority to enforce all three offenses because alcohol, drugs and prostitution go hand and hand with liquor violations.

The biggest change for our department and the state was that "liquor by the drink" was finally passed in about four counties in North Carolina. As everyone knows, laws do not stop people from breaking laws, and the liquor houses and illegal clubs would continue on. Our job would become more complex. Now we had to interview prospective licensees for the sale of liquor in approved establishments, and educate the potential licensee in the laws and regulations regarding their new license.

One day as I was going about my regular duties, I received a distressing call from my mother. Snoopy had died. He had not been neutered, (Bob Barker, I wish you had started your plea earlier.) and had gone to see some female about a mile away. A car hit him and when my father went to find him, he found his body on the side of the road.

I immediately drove to their house, and we had a service and buried him on a lot they owned next to their house. I felt so guilty and wished that I could have seen him one more time. Actually, many people did not have their dogs neutered and spayed at this time. I am not making excuses, but it was a while before I ever owned a dog again. I returned to my apartment, sad and angry with myself. I was to work the weekend, but my mind was somewhere else.

The following Monday, I received word that I was to attend "Rookie" school. It was a new requirement for all law enforcement officers. The classes were six hours per day for six weeks, and were to be given in a small town about forty miles away from Charlotte. I knew that it was understood that I would continue to work my scheduled weekends and any undercover assignments, "Rookie" school or not.

Interstate 77 had just been finished, so the trip would be cut in half, but I still tried all of my persuasive techniques to talk JB out of making me go. I knew that he really did not have any control over it, but I had to give it my best shot.

About 10 days before I was to start class, JB came to me and asked if I would mind if a young female deputy sheriff could ride with me. I said, "Absolutely not. I do not want any female deputy riding with me."

After about an hour, he came into my office and said that the Sheriff had called the Raleigh office and, in lieu of county budget cuts, we needed to carpool. I said I wanted to meet this girl first, and if I had to babysit her, I would, but I was not going to ride in any marked car. I already knew I would hate the girl and never speak to her. If she did not like my music, she could wear earplugs.

She, whom I dubbed "Deputy Daugh," and I met for coffee next door to my office. When she walked in I knew I was going to hate her. I could tell that she was as much of a bitch as I was. She was about 5'5" and weighed about a hundred pounds. I could close my eyes and just imagine "Mutt and Jeff."

I was 5'10" (over 6" with heels) and big boned. She sat down and we talked. She brought up the car situation and explained to me that she did not have an assigned car. On the days she was to drive, she would have to drive into Charlotte, pick up a car and then pick me up.

I told her that I would be driving every day. I gave her directions to my apartment so she could drive to my house, and then I would drive the two of us to the school. She left and I went back to my office trying to think of the excuse I was going to give JB. I decided that I did not work for the county, so screw the county and their budget.

When I returned to the office, I informed JB that I would be driving every day. I explained "Deputy Daugh's" car situation and the fact that the state currently owed me about four months of "comp" time, and this way would be more efficient. Before he had time to figure out what I had just said, I left.

The first day of school was finally here. I waited outside of my apartment for "DD' to arrive. (I did not want her in my apartment.) When she finally arrived, we immediately left. The car was silent except for my 60s music. After about thirty-five minutes, "DD" started talking about nothing in particular, and I drove faster and faster.

When we arrived at our destination I quickly parked, jumped out of the car and rushed into the building. When I walked into the squad room, at least thirty heads turned at once and they all smiled. I smiled back.

Naturally, all were male and the only difference was that of their age and physical condition. This was just like my office, except the guys in my office were all under thirty-five and basically in great shape. The room was arranged with about ten tables and only two empty seats remained. Just my luck, I would have to sit beside "DD." That is if she ever made it from the car. She finally entered and heads turned again, and smiles were returned again.

For about an hour, each of us introduced ourselves and talked about what type of work we did in law enforcement. The class was better than I had expected and concentrated on actual field experience.

Lunch break came and I was nice. I asked "DD" if she wanted to go to a restaurant, but she told me that she had brought her lunch. I knew she had a small bag with her when she got in my car, but I never thought it contained her lunch. I could not believe it! Who in the hell would bring their own lunch? I told her that we had passed a picnic area on our way in, and she said that would be fine. Off we went before any of the guys saw her lunch bag. About the time she finished her meal and I finished my drink, several of the guys walked by and stopped to talk with us. They all seemed nice and "DD" walked back with them.

The next couple of days during our drive were exactly as the first. "DD" did start a conversation and told me that she had two children, was a single mother and hated the fact that she had to carry a gun. I proceeded to ask her why she chose law enforcement, and she stated that the sheriff's department paid more than her other job.

About a week later I started talking to her, and we were civil from then on. After the next couple of weeks, anyone seeing us would have thought we were friends. On one occasion, she invited me over to meet her children. The children were ok, as far as children go. I have never been a maternal person, and never in a million years, picture myself with children. I did decide that "DD" had a lot on her plate and not much money to fill it up.

For the remainder of the school, I told her that I would drive to her house and pick her up in order to help her save on gas. She really seemed to appreciate this. Her office was not reimbursing her for gas or food. I saw her children almost every day when I dropped her off. I began to like them and realize that "DD" was a really good mother, and always placed their needs before her own, which I would never be able to do. We continued our routine of going to school every day, but now we were talking and laughing and the drive seemed shorter and shorter. She loved beach music, so she could not be all that bad.

The technique of role-playing was involved in most exercises we performed during our classes. I did well with the mock interrogations, interviews, arrest procedures and court situations. "DD' took twice as much time as I did, but the end result was the same. Maybe I was not as confident as I thought I was.

There were some exercises we could only do alone. I remember one day we were placed in a dark room to practice with pop-up figures. Anyone reading this story that has seen TV or movies about the police, should have some familiarity with this procedure. If not, figures can be that of a bank robber, a woman holding a child, a school bus, another police officer, etc. The figures pop up rapidly, and you have to decide which one to shoot and which one not to shoot. "DD" was the only person that made a perfect score. I, on the other hand, shot all but one pop-up. My excuse, and I always had one, was it was better to be safe than sorry.

Here was "DD," who was totally disinterested in law enforcement, and performed better than any other law enforcement officer in the class—even seasoned guys. I did not know about the others, but I was humbled.

Qualifying on the range was saved until last. Since I was about eight years old and received my first shotgun, a Fox Sterlingworth 410, my love and respect for all firearms began. I knew I was an excellent marksman and was really looking forward to going to the range.

The day before we were to qualify, we were told by the instructor not to bring a loaded gun to the range. To further emphasize, he explained that he would check all guns at the range, and if one gun were loaded, all the class would automatically fail the course. No exceptions.

When I picked up "DD" that next morning, we both unloaded our guns and placed the bullets on the floor mats. "DD" was dressed in dress pants and I was dressed in the attire I always wore on raids: jeans and my western style holster and my six inch Smith and Weston.

As I was driving on I77, about three or four mile before crossing over the Lake Norman Bridge, a car flew by me going in excess of a hundred miles an hour. I realized the car had out of state tags and two men with very long hair were seated in the back seat. I picked up the mike on my state radio to call the highway patrol, and told "DD" to fasten her seat belt. For some unknown reason, I was unable to reach any highway patrolman.

As I was closing in on the speeding car, with my faulty blue light flickering on and off, the other car dead stopped in the middle of the bridge. I continued to fly past them. By the time I was completely stopped, I was about a mile passed the other car. I backed up and pulled behind the car. I told "DD" to try any channel on the radio for assistance.

Before I got out of my car I told "DD" to lock the doors, and if anything happened, to drive off. When I exited my car, the driver of the other car quickly exited his. I noticed his hand moving toward the small of his back. I immediately went for my gun, but in the background, I heard "DD" yell, "Bullets!" In that millisecond I realized two things: my bullets were on the floorboard, and I would probably die on this day.

As it turned out, the guy was going for his ID and badge. He identified himself as a Federal Marshal and I identified myself as a State ALE agent without missing a beat. He explained to me he was transporting prisoners and apologized for speeding. I told him to be careful and watch the speed limit.

After he walked back to his car and drove off, I turned and walked toward mine. As I got closer to the car, I noticed that "DD" had her gun drawn and it was pointed toward where the marshal's car had been parked. As I got in the car, she put her gun down, unloaded it and started shaking. It was about twenty years before we ever spoke of this incident. Even twenty years was too soon for me.

Everyone completed the course, we were furnished lunch and all the guys promised to keep in touch. I never saw or heard from them again. Of course, I never contacted them either.

The following Monday I returned to my office and was informed that I was to begin another undercover campaign in the county where I was burned. I went to the same liquor houses and actually bought from the same guy that shot out my back window.

The city police department and the county sheriff department had warrants drawn, and we raided the illegal establishments. We used officers from both departments, and we confiscated enough beer and liquor to fill the entire parking lot and the entire front of the sheriff's department. The sheriff informed me that his county had not had a sting operation in over five years.

The chief of detectives for the city had asked me out when I started my last campaign, but I really did not want to become involved at that time. After the campaign was complete, I decided to take him up on his offer. Spending so much time around other law enforcement personnel, I guess it was only natural for me to become involved with a fellow professional.

Sam had been separated for about six months after being married sixteen years without children. During the separation, his wife had evidently become pregnant by the sheriff from a neighboring county. Sam explained to me that he had no intention of going back with his wife and had filed for divorce.

I was an old hand with hearing the separation story. I decided to use my investigative skills and check things out. I check out where his wife worked, and found out that she was living with her parents in a town about fifteen miles away from where Sam lived. During my initial mini investigation of her, I learned she was the personnel director of the largest company in the county and always interviewed all applicants personally.

I visited her work place, completed a job application and waited to be interviewed. I knew when she interviewed me that I would slowly take control of the situation and end up interviewing her. She never realized when I had taken control. She openly told me all the personal specifics of her failed marriage and some facts I really did not want to know. When she offered me a job, I explained to her that I would let her know within the week. I wondered how many times she attempted to call the number of the Chinese restaurant I had used as a contact number.

I felt as though Sam had been honest with me and decided to continue our relationship. Sam loved to fish and had a boat. I had a friend with a beach house, so we would go to Myrtle Beach on our free most weekends. I always referred to our mini vacations as the "The Three F's." Sam had many assets, but most important, he loved sex.

Thank goodness for the sexual revolution, and the changes in people's attitudes about sex, which the sixties had brought about for women. Single women could have numerous sexual partners and finally enjoy the freedom, without embarrassment, that men had always had. Even younger married women could openly talk about sex, the "Big O" and demand more from their spouses.

After all of my court dates were completed in Sam's county, he asked me to marry him. He was a great guy and I loved our time together, but I was not particularly interested in a permanent relationship.

As it came closer to the delivery date for his wife, I wondered what might happen. He was at my apartment when his friend called and informed him that the baby had been born. He did not seem very interested until his in-laws called and asked him to come to the hospital—big mistake.

He called later and said that his wife refused to take care of the baby and planned on moving back into her parent's house. While at the hospital and after seeing the baby, he decided to take leave from his job and take on the responsibility of caring for the baby—bigger mistake. He immediately hired a nanny to help out, but he had bonded with the child, whom the wife named after him prior to him getting to the hospital. We continued to date and he was still talking about marriage. I did not.

I had changed only one diaper in my life, and never did master, nor did I want to, how to get the clean diaper on the baby. Sam was up for anything I wanted to do. I knew that he had never been dancing or attended a concert. I took him to see The Tams, The Cavaliers and other groups. Teaching him to shag presented too many problems and took too much time away from our more important activities.

He introduced me to gospel and bluegrass music. Gospel was music I had never heard, but I loved the deep voices of the singers. Our life was going well, but I knew my job was just too demanding, and soon I would be sent to work with the feds. He was familiar with the demands of law enforcement and understood my time away.

Soon I began my campaign with the feds and was out of town for weeks at a time. Working with the feds was much different than working for the state, but in positive ways. I did find out early on, after working with other federal agencies, that I did not want to pursue a career with the FBI.

A person can always tell an FBI agent from the other feds. They are what I call, "Hooverized." All wore dark suits, white shirts, black wing tips and plain ties. Of course, not so long ago all FBI agents were CPAs and lawyers. Don't get me wrong, I had friends in the bureau and respect then and the job they do. The agents with the federal agencies I worked with were more relaxed and not so stiff.

It was an asset for me to rely on my past life experiences and the effect that living in the sixties prepared me for. I still felt invincible; therefore, any assignment given me, I entered with my usual zest and "full steam ahead" attitude.

As I was traveling to so many different cites and places, it was difficult to keep up with where I was and where I had been. I kept a tape recorder in my hotel room. After returning to my room, I would dictate the descriptions of the people I dealt with, the surroundings I visited and which illegal activities I observed. After completing each tape, I would mail it to the appropriate federal office.

As I dealt almost exclusively with males, being a female naturally worked to my advantage. There were times I had to play the role of the helpless female. This was the hardest role for me to play.

Working with federal laws was so different than state laws. Federal laws were much easier on the agent than state laws. When I worked alcohol cases, I never had to carry an evidence bottle to prove I purchased liquor, and I only had to witness the prostitution to prove my case. The gambling was different.

I had always been lucky with gambling during my undercover assignments. As the state of feds provided the money, they were entitled to the profits. After a couple of days, I told them to give me twenty dollars per night, (this way the legal issue was resolved) and after I gambled their money away, I would switch to my own and keep the profits.

Many times it was dangerous and inconvenient for me to carry a gun. Where was I to put it when I wore a short, tight and strapless cocktail dress? I was still teaching self defense, and I felt confident in my skills and hoped that I could handle myself.

After I had gathered enough information, warrants were issued. It was time for the raids—my favorite part. With the assistance of about one hundred agents, we raided about sixty places simultaneously. I was driven to each place to make identifications and make arrests. I ended up using my Miranda Warning "cheat card" instead of saying it from memory. I did not want any of these people to get off on a technicality.

The worst place, and the one that was believed to be the most trouble, was kept until last. When we arrived, the two steel doors (which we already knew were three feet thick and fifteen feet high) were closed. Someone had arranged for a bulldozer with a battering ram. (You got to love the feds) The agent in charge called the owner, identified himself, and told him he had a warrant and instructed him to open the doors or we would. The owner hung up on the agent in charge.

We waited five minutes and rammed the door. When the dust settled, the hundred of us with pistols and shotguns already drawn, rushed in. We were met with as many sawed off shotguns, assault rifles and automatic weapons than I had ever seen. (They had better weapons than we did.) For just a second, it turned into a stand off until the owner noticed the snipers. He lowered his weapon and motioned for his gang to lower theirs. I guess he, like us, did not want to die.

All of the guys, except the four assigned to guard me, gathered the arsenal and the bad guys. The agent in charge served the owner with the warrants, and I stepped forward to make my identifications. When I pointed to a female behind the bar, the owner literally jumped over the bar and ran toward me. I noticed a pistol in his hand, but by the time he reached me, I had already drawn my gun and was ready to do what I was trained to do. Fortunately, my guardian angels saw the gun at the same time I had and stopped him in his tracks. He called me a lying, GD bitch as he was being escorted out. The woman I identified ended up being his wife.

The guy in question had been arrested many times, but not by the feds. In the past, he had managed to always obtain a good attorney and walk away with a stiff fine. Now he was facing major liquor violations, serious gun charges and the assault on a federal officer. (When I, as a state agent, worked with the feds, I carried the same jurisdiction as they did.)

All of the cases were lumped together, and because they were in the same federal jurisdiction, were heard by one judge. All were found guilty. The case against the wife of the man mentioned above was dismissed before it ever got to court. It was decided, since her twin sister had come forward and confessed to being the person who sold to me, to drop the case against the original defendant. I demanded a lie detector test, but the agent in charge explained to me that her husband was facing active time and a $200,000 fine, and that satisfied the government. It did not satisfy me, but I knew that there would be another time and another place.

One of my cases never went to federal court. The defendant was indisposed. He had placed dynamite in the car of the sheriff of his county and at the sheriff's home. Both charges went off, but no one was killed. There was a tremendous amount of property damage. This was the same guy who owned the club that JB had sent the young patrolman in to find me.

The guy was really nice when we raided his club. He offered us a seat and told us to help ourselves to anything from behind the bar. (He really was not smart enough to be witty.) As he read the warrant, he glance at me and announced to everyone that he had never sold liquor to any law enforcement person before. (which was true) He then proceeded to tell everyone that he could never turn down a pretty city girl. This was no compliment, as he had never been to a city and never had seen a "girl" who wasn't missing teeth. Although his reputation for violence was well known, he was actually the most docile person I have ever arrested.

I went to an indoor range on a regular basis and really enjoyed it. One of my fellow agents, The Wild Card, loved the range as much as I did. I had purchased a couple of pistols but always wanted more. Wild Card told me of a police supply store in a neighboring county and said that they had better prices. We went together and I purchased an S&W 42 Magnum nickel-plated. I signed the registration, and we shopped some more and then left.

About five weeks later, the local ATF (Alcohol Tax and Firearms) called me and asked me to come into their office. I knew all the agents well and had done some work for them. When I entered the office, they explained to me that I would have to apply for a federal firearms license if I continued to buy firearms. I explained to them that I had bought about three since being with the state. They produced papers showing that I had bought twenty-five from different counties and states. I stared at them with a confused look on my face (I have mastered this look) and said, "No way."

They showed me receipts and asked if the signature was mine. As I was looking over them, I recognized one as mine. The others were written in the familiar handwriting of Wild Card. Not only had he forged my name, he had misspelled it. The agents told me they knew that my actual signature was only on one registration, but that did not change the legal issue. Once a person buys a firearm, the registration remains in the original buyer's name. If someone committed a crime twenty-five years in the future with one of the other twenty-four pistols, it would come back in my lap. I said, "Ok, how do we fix the forgery issue?"

Since the owner of the gun store was working with Wild Card, both had to be prosecuted, and I was to be the only witness for the government. How could this person, a fellow agent, do this to me? I looked up at my ATF friends and said something to the effect, "Burn the bastard and let me light the fire." The only thing that I was uncomfortable with was not being able to discuss this with JB.

The ATF did their job as usual. When they raided Wild Card's mother's home, more firearms and priceless one of a kind weapons were found than had ever been found in a private residence. Naturally, Wild Card testified against the owner of the gun store. I never saw Wild Card again, but I understood that he took a job as chief of security for his grandfather's company in "a land far, far away." As always, wealth does have its privileges. In about three weeks, a new agent was transferred to our office. He looked like a body builder, dressed great and his expression was very serious.

As I am the type of person who says what I think, and I expect the same out of everyone else, JB decided that the new agent and I would work as partners for two weekends a month. I noticed all of the other agents had shocked looks on their faces, but I was even more surprised when I found out later that the look was not of shock. The other agents were jealous of the new agent's accessibility to me. They had made a bet with each other, the first day they met me, as to who would be the first to have sex with me. Men!

I nicknamed the new agent, "Hoss" after the character in *Bonanza*. We started working together and immediately formed a bond. Hoss had been in law enforcement for several years. Currently, he worked for the same department I did before being transferred to my office. We worked together perfectly and I knew immediately that if there were any trouble, I could depend on him as I could depend on the rest of the guys. Besides, Hoss had the best looking service revolver I had ever placed in my hands, a S&W nickel plated 9MM. God, how I love guns!

On one of the weekends in which Hoss and I were working, I decided to drive by an apartment complex in my assigned area. The day before I had received a tip that the complex was selling liquor illegally and that a big party was planned the following night. We drove by about 1:50 AM and noticed the only lights we could see were in the direction of the clubhouse.

We parked, walked around the main building, noticed empty beer and liquor bottles on the lawn, and noticed several people who were obviously intoxicated. We decided to enter the clubhouse and see what was happening. There was no one posted at the front to ask us for identification (This clubhouse operated as a private club.) to enter. We entered the foyer, and by this time we could hear music blaring. Well, this was enough of an invitation, as I needed. I told Hoss that we would go in and observe what was happening.

There was a large bar with one guy resting his head on it. About thirty liquor bottles were on top of the bar. We noticed two entrances that were covered with heavy curtains. Except for about ten people, the place was empty. This was really strange.

I walked up to the bar and ordered a drink. The man I had seen earlier lifted his head off the bar, and when he stood he was taller than JB. He said some sexual remarks and told me to get what I wanted. I started to walk away when the curtains parted on the door about sixty feet away, and at least 150 people entered. I walked about ten feet from the bar and told Hoss to go to the car and call for backup.

The guy at the bar came over to me and put his arm around my shoulder. Before I could do anything, he felt my gun, pushed me against the bar and pinned me behind the bar up against the wall. I told him that I was a state ALE officer, and he looked down and saw my badge clipped to my waistband. He released me for just a moment, but not long enough for me to reach for my nightstick. He grabbed my hand and twisted my thumb until it was dislocated. Instinct and pain took over and I attempted to knee him in the gonads. Before I could make contact, Hoss came from out of nowhere, grabbed the bastard and pushed him away from me. They both fell against the other curtain and crashed through, not a wooden door, a sliding glass door.

As the heavy curtain protected me and everyone else from the glass, I carefully walked through the opening and saw that Hoss had overpowered the guy and that the barrel of his 9mm was rammed down the guy's throat. I walked over to Hoss and said something to the effect of "Not here and not now." As he was pulling his gun out of the guy's throat, I handcuffed the bastard. As I was in the process of frisking him, I discovered a switchblade and an ankle holster. As I disarmed him, I saw about thirty city policemen in the process of crowd control give me a thumbs up.

The city police had to call a bus to transport all the drunks and all the liquor. I told the sergeant to take the credit for the arrest and he thanked me. We took our time transporting the assailant to jail.

I waited for JB to call the following day, but he never did. Now I knew that I was no longer newsworthy. When I arrived on Monday, JB was waiting in his car. I did not even go into the office. I just opened the passenger side of the door and slid into the seat. We drove off and when he stopped, he asked what had happened on Sunday. I explained exactly what had transpired and that Hoss had acted appropriately.

He then told me that he had not been exactly forthcoming regarding Hoss' past. I just looked at him, He continued to explain to me that while in the line of duty, Hoss had shot and killed one man and seriously injured another. He further told me that he had been cleared on both charges and that he was transferred to our office to determine if he should be allowed to continue in law enforcement. After much deliberation with the Raleigh office, it was decided that I was to be assigned as his partner to evaluate how he performed in the field.

I just burst out laughing. When I regained my composure, I asked him if he were kidding and if he really did not know me by now. I have always been known as a hot head, a "know it all," a person who acts and speaks without thinking and who has an uncontrollable temper. This time he laughed. He said, "Yes, but as long as you have been working in this job, you have maintained control of that temper and have had a calming affect on the other agents." I had never been described as having a calming effect on anyone.

This did not change the fact that, in my opinion, Hoss acted as any good officer would when his partner was being threatened. I know that men possess the natural instinct to protect a female. I am a product of the sixties, I marched for equality and I believe strongly in the Equal Rights Amendment. But when a male, who is physically stronger, overpowers a female, it can be a lifesaver for another man to be around, especially when he carries a gun. I forgot I was not going to discuss my political beliefs.

When I returned to the office, all agents were there. As I sat down at my desk, I realized I had not said anything to JB as to why he had not called me about the incident over the weekend. Oh well, such is life. All the guys asked about my thumb and stated they were glad that I was ok. I actually did work with the best group of guys in the state or anywhere else.

JB came into our offices and asked what had happened to my hand, sneaky man that he is, and then informed me that I was to take time off. This was a mandatory request and before I could contest it, he looked at his watch and said, "Go now," and pointed to the door. I left wondering how the office would make it without me.

I called my parents and told them that I was on extended leave. My father suggested that he wanted to give my sister and me a vacation. As my sister and I had never gotten along, I wondered what my father was thinking. Maybe a "bonding" experience?

I knew that my sister would think up as many reasons to back out as I would. My father had always given me, and I guess her, everything. He was the type of father that you never had to ask for anything, he just gave. The next day he called and had made all of the arrangements for my sister and I to go on a four day cruise to the Bahamas and a three-day vacation in Vegas.

I really do not know where Sandy was living, but we met at the Miami Airport and then took a taxi to the port. When we boarded the ship and were taken to our room, Sandy commented on the fact that our room, which had a balcony overlooking the water, was large for a cruise ship. As I had never been on a cruise ship, I took her word for it.

Evidently, Dad had arranged for us to have the 8:00 PM dinner seating. Our dinner companions were two gay men. I wondered if good old dad had arranged that also. I had never tasted such wonderful and unusual food. Sandy on the other hand, had lived abroad and really enjoyed and recognized different foods.

Although I had fought a weight problem all my life, real food and real meals were not my problem. When I was a minor and lived at home, I had to eat everything on my plate before I could eat dessert. When I turned 18 and was legally an adult, I only consumed sweets, snacks, liquor and appetizers.

As the ship contained several gambling casinos, I was content to gamble the night away. One of the people at my black jack table was one of our dinner companions. He, like I, loved to gamble. Unfortunately, he was either a much better gambler or luckier than me. I just did not know when to quit, and I like so many gamblers, always thought I would win back my losses.

When the morning of the second day arrived, I decided I did not want the confinement of the ship. To me, the passengers seemed to be led around and told what to do. We were already told when to eat and the silly cruise director was always flitting around and talking about planned tours. As I am a control freak, I didn't think I could take much more.

That afternoon when we docked in Nassau, Sandy and I were the first ones to disembark. (with our bathing suits) Evidently, venturing out on our own did not seem to bother her either.

As we were walking around, I noticed many familiar sites, and it brought back memories of DJ and our times in Nassau and several of the surrounding islands. I kept thinking that I might see her. What a reunion that would have been! Unfortunately, I did not see DJ or any of the other people I had met and partied with on so many occasions.

A taxi driver stopped and asked us if we wanted a ride around the island. We negotiated a price for the day, and off we went. He took us to places that only the natives would know about. He drove us to a private beach with a breathtaking view. We told him to stop in order for us to shop, swim and snorkel. We spent the rest of the day doing what we wanted. After a couple of hours Sandy was ready to get in the shade, but I, a sun worshiper, stayed on the beach. Sandy has red hair, very fair complexion and favors our mother's side of the family. I favor my father's side and that is not our only difference. Our general appearances and personalities are as opposite as night and day.

Evidently, our taxi driver and Sandy met as she was walking toward an umbrella, and he introduced her to a friend of his. The friend was a medical student, and they asked her if they could be our escorts for the night. By the time I arrived, the plans were confirmed. They were to pick us up at the ship about 8:00 PM, show us the island nightlife, have drinks, hear steel drums and take in a play at Fort Charlotte. I was totally agreeable. After all, who can turn down an invitation from two nice guys who speak with a British accent?

A couple of hours later, we returned to the ship to shower and change clothes. At 8:00 PM on the dot our escorts were waiting at the end of the gangplank They took us to about ten local bars where we drank, listened to the unusual sound of steel drums, (this was a first for me) danced, shared a couple of joints and had a great time.

About midnight, we left to go to Fort Charlotte. The crowd was not very large and soon lights and music could be heard everywhere. I could not see any actors, and I learned that the performance involved only sound and light. (another first for me) The show and view of the lights as they reflected off the Caribbean, was beyond belief. Of course, the moon shining on the water added to the beauty. After the performance, we left to enjoy more nightlife. We returned to the ship about mid afternoon with an invitation for a repeat performance of the night before.

Back on board, we took a catnap and prepared for the night's adventure. The guys took us to different clubs, but this night we were also invited to the med student's home for drinks and numerous sea delicacies. His family was very gracious, and after eating we were taken to several more clubs to listen to the steel drums and talk. As the saying goes, "It was a good time had by all." The trip just didn't last long enough.

The next day, I tried my hand at gambling again. This time, I was less lucky than the last. Before I could leave for Vegas, I had to stop by the local Amex office to get funds for the rest of my trip.

We left Nassau, stayed in Miami for a few days and then left for Vegas. We stayed at the MGM Grand (before the fire) and attended shows featuring Tom Jones, Wayne Newton, and tributes to The Beatles and The Rat Pack. We also saw comedy shows with Steve Martin and Rodney Dangerfield. After the shows we gambled and walked the strip.

The following day, (like, who knows the difference) we rented a car and drove to the Hoover Dam, saw Lake Mead and on into Arizona. One day, I contacted the Nevada Gaming Commission and made an appointment for a job interview. There were no openings, but I enjoyed seeing their set up.

I asked a dealer where the entertainers went when they came to Vegas, and I was told that Paul Anka had a club called Jubilation and we went that night. It must have been an off night, but we did see signed pictures of everyone that was anyone.

One of the many things I loved about Vegas was looking out the hotel window and seeing the snow covered mountains in the distance, and knowing that the temperature outside our hotel was over 100 degrees. I loved the climate and could have settled there but all good things have to end sometime.

When it was time to leave, we took a limo to the airport and ran into Buddy Hackett as he was arriving. We left in separation directions, Sandy going to St. Louis, and I to Charlotte. Although we both seemed to have a nice time, it was over twenty-five years before we actually spoke again.

When I arrived in Charlotte, Sam was waiting at the gate. He had his boat on the trailer and we left, with another couple, for Myrtle Beach. Sam and I decided to go fishing by ourselves and caught nothing but small stingrays, which we carefully threw back in the water. When Sam attempted to start the boat, it wouldn't start. We sat there, about six miles from shore, waiting for someone with a large enough boat to tow us. About an hour later, with the sun setting in the west, a guy came by and offered to tow us. I was glad when those three days were over. The combination of jet lag, no sleep, drinking and smoking was too much for me.

When we returned to Charlotte, Sam had to go home, have the motor checked out and run the motor in fresh water. We had gotten shrimp before we left the beach and I could not wait to boil them. But first things first: turn on the stereo, pour myself a vodka with a slice of fresh lime, make my famous cocktail sauce, boil the shrimp and light a joint. After about an hour I decided that the situation called for playing the soundtrack of "Easy Rider." Of course, this called for another joint. I was sorry I had no one with me to sing, "Don't Bogart That Joint, My Friend," so I had to grin and bare it and had to sing alone. I had no plans for the next few days but to "veg out" and enjoy myself.

Eventually I had to return to the real world. Before I had left on vacation, I had been assigned a new car with the full police package. As I was sitting at my desk the following Monday morning, I received a call from a local strip club owner. He wanted me to be first to know that he had booked the "Chippendales," an all male group, to perform the next

Saturday at one of his clubs. He explained all about the group, and after we hung up I realized, **payback had finally come!**

I told JB that I would be glad to work the following weekend and could I take all of the other agents with me. He was about to object, so I had to tell him about the Chippendales and that it was about time I got my payback. He just smiled and said that I could drive three guys and he would drive the other four. JB always liked a good prank. Eventually, he told the guys that all of us were going to assist in a raid with the feds.

I contacted several of my girl friends, Liz, Pattie, Martha, Chandelier, "DD" and Ginger. I told them to meet me at the club that Saturday at about 8:30pm and that they were to be my guests. When I explained what was up and that I had arranged for all of us to stay the weekend at the hotel next door, I could hear them packing.

When we arrived at the club, JB instructed the other guys to station themselves around the dance floor. I sat down at a table with my friends and waited. When the bright lights came on, and the music started, and all the women started screaming, I could see the expression of "What the hell?" on the faces of my fellow agents. Not only were they the only male patrons, they were directly beside the stage.

When the dancers entered, it took them only a second to realize not only what I had done, but that they didn't have keys to the cars and couldn't leave. They all moved to the back of the lounge and stood with their backs to the walls. As I had already made plans with the owner, the male dancers went up to the male agents and shook their stuff. This was almost as enjoyable as the show. My good friend and fellow agent, JL, always pulled his pants up when he was nervous, and his pants were about as far up as they would go. Any higher and he could have done some serious damage to himself.

The Chippendales became regulars in Charlotte, and I never missed a show. When it was my scheduled weekend to work, I always took my partners. They, like me at the topless clubs, never got over their awkwardness. I had much to get even for. Not just for the topless bars, or the times they would take me the biggest red neck places in the world, in hopes that I would get into a "cat fight," but also taking me to gay clubs and walking out on me. I told them that I am a Gemini and we always hold grudges and get even and that I was only beginning to get even with them!

My birthday was just around the corner, and I knew that Michael would be calling soon. I did not have to wait long. He called and wanted to take me out to supper. I told him that I really did not want to see him again. Then he told me that he had someone he wanted me to meet. I told him I would meet him and his friend at one of my favorite restaurants, Victoria Station.

I arrived early, found a seat in one of the train cars and ordered a drink. Michael entered followed by one of the most distinguished older men I had ever seen. Michael made the introductions, and when the man bowed and kissed my hand, I was pleasantly surprised.

The next week, Adam called and asked if I wanted to go out for drinks, and I agreed. Over drinks I explained to him that I was not interested in having a sexual relationship, and he told me that he wasn't either. We went to plays, movies and on many weekend outings on his boat. He was interesting to talk with and we had a purely platonic relationship. This was nice for a change.

He was the second man with whom I had a relationship, who had strong ties to the Mafia. Adam was a great guy and I enjoyed our times together, but I had to be careful with whom I associated. I do not think the feds would appreciate, understand or believe this relationship, whether platonic or not. I definitely was not going to put myself in the impossible position of being expected to "turn him." Yeah, like he would turn. Sadly, we slowly drifted apart.

As Sam was trying to juggle a baby and his job, I would only see him on my off weekends and when I would visit him. He was continuing to talk of marriage, but I knew and he did also, what my feelings about children were.

One night, as I was talking on the phone, my call waiting clicked in. I never learned how to use it without cutting off the person I was talking to, so I did not answer it. The damn thing kept clicking in, and after about forty-five minutes my doorbell rang. I went downstairs and when I opened the door, JB was standing there. He told me that my father had had a heart attack and I was to leave immediately for the hospital. He asked if he could drive me and I told him I appreciated the offer, but I would drive myself.

I left immediately for the hospital. When I arrived at the hospital, I found my mother in the intensive care unit waiting room. I spoke with his doctor and was informed Daddy's situation was grave.

The doctor went into Daddy's room to inform him that I had arrived. Daddy told the doctor he wanted to see me. I prepared myself for the worst, but as I entered the room Daddy was sitting up in bed with his usual smile. We talked, and I mentioned that I had his Model 1897 Winchester that was given him by his father, reblued. His smile got even larger, and he asked me to bring it by in the morning in order for him to see what kind of job the gunsmith had done. When my ten minutes were over, I left the room.

Immediately, I drove back to my apartment, put the Winchester in its case and drove back to the hospital. As I walked in the front door, a security guard stopped and told me that I could not bring a gun into the hospital. I glanced at him, pulled back my jacket in order for him to see both my badge and my "38" and continued on. When I reached the nurses station, I asked if I could go see my father. They told me to go right in.

My father looked around, saw the case and shook his head. I opened the case and showed the gun to him. He looked it over and told me that the gunsmith who blued the gun was a real professional. We talked a little more until my time was over. I picked up the gun and told him that I would be back for the next visitation. This was the last time I ever saw my father alive.

Everybody handles devastating situations differently. I had never shown much emotional feelings; therefore, I handled his death my way. I decided to take charge of any arrangements. This was a little difficult as my mother was also very dogmatic. I finally had to back off and just let her take over.

When we received guests at the funeral home, three hours turned into six before we could leave. My parents belonged to a large Methodist church that could accommodate almost two thousand people. When we arrived, I noticed that there was at least that many people standing outside and in the street in front of the church, in the snow. Large speakers were arranged in order for everyone to be able to hear the service.

My father was respected and beloved by everyone. He gave of his time to the community willingly. He started Little League baseball in our county and ran the organization (I mean he and my mother were at every game working the concession and fixing hotdogs) for at least twenty years. He demanded that every coach allow all the young boys on each team to play, whether they were good players or not.

He gave free golf lessons to ladies in the entire county at the city recreation center. He did not do this just to teach golf, but for his love of the game. If someone came into his store and didn't have enough money to purchase what they needed, he would make up the difference. Many times he would give the merchandise to them, especially if the child was in need. To this day, there is a ladies only golf tournament given in his memory and honor, and the Little League field still bears his name.

I had never really thought completely seriously about getting married until after his death. As he had always been the dominant male figure in my life, I never felt the need to marry. As my friend, Liz, was riding with me back to my apartment to pick up some things, I turned to her and said, "I'll be married in six months." Liz never replied because she knew me well enough to know that I would indeed, be married within six months. Unfortunately, one of my major liabilities has always been to act on the spur of the moment and without thinking about the consequences.

I decided I needed some R&R and since a long weekend was approaching, I decided to travel to Savannah, Georgia for St. Patrick's Day. Savannah, Georgia has the best St. Patrick's Day celebration. The city closes for about three days. Nobody is arrested, everybody is Irish, the parades are fantastic and all the water in the fountains is dyed green. You can have Boston and New York, and I have been to all three, but Savannah is still the best. I called Chandelier and told her that I was coming.

After I arrived, she told me that there was a new club that offered beach music and live entertainment. That night, after arriving at the club and dancing for about two hours straight, we went back to our seats and ordered another drink. A guy came over and started talking to Chandelier, asked her to dance and then asked if he could sit at our table. Lou seemed interested in Chandelier, but I could tell she was not interested in him.

He left the table, but the next time I was on the dance floor he cut in. We talked and learned that our birthdays were both on May 29th, but he was a year older than I. His father had recently died in February, just as mine had. Things proceeded and he asked me if I would be interested in spending our birthdays together. I agreed and we exchanged telephone numbers.

When I returned to Charlotte, Lou called me every night and "talked the talk," and I should have "walked the walk." He came to Charlotte to visit every weekend. He did meet my criteria. He loved sex and could not get enough of it, and he would do anything to please me. After about three months, he asked me to marry him. He really was not the type of man I usually dated, but I was vulnerable.

As I was still in regular contact with both Sam and Grant, I decided to weigh my options. Sam came to Daddy's funeral and supported me through this trying time. Grant had called the day he heard Daddy died, and came to visit me with a wonderful card and flowers in hand.

I called Grant first, as he will always be the only man that I will ever be in love with. I asked him to meet me the following night. We met and I told him that I knew we loved each other and always would, but I needed to know if there was a future for us now. He told me that he always wanted to be an active part of his children's lives and to see them daily, but he also wanted the same with me. We both knew that I was just too selfish to share him and that if we married, we would probably end up hating each other. We decided to part as friends.

The next day I contacted Sam, and we had a similar discussion. He had bonded with the baby and found out that he loved being a daddy. He knew that I would never accept the child and never wanted any children of my own. He was correct on both counts; therefore, we also parted friends.

Was I stupid? Yes.

Chapter 4

"His Mother Should Have Thrown Him Out and Kept the Stork' ~ May West

Lou and I were married six months later. As I had not attended a church since I turned eighteen, I felt it hypocritical to marry in one. We were married in my parent's home with only family and close friends in attendance at the ceremony. Sandy was my Maid of Honor, and I wore the same wedding dress my great grandmother had worn in 1855. The reception was wonderful, and I had so much fun that I really did not want to leave. I guess all good things must come to an end.

Lou had lost his job in Savannah and a friend of mine had offered him a job to take over the territory in Richmond, Virginia. I knew Lou could not sell coal in hell, but I could sell ice in Alaska. I knew that my friend had offered the job because of our friendship.

We spent the first night of our honeymoon in Charlotte at a hotel one of my friends owned, and he comped the room. The band at the lounge that night was the Embers, and we shagged and toasted until about 3:00 AM. For once in my life, I was more concerned with starting our honeymoon that listening to beach music. I kept wondering and asking Lou when we were going back to the room, and he kept putting it off. Considering what great sex we experienced before marriage, I knew that the sex inside of the marriage would be just as satisfying or more so.

As it turned out, I was so wrong. What I should have done the next day was visit an attorney and have the marriage annulled. I told Lou my plans and he said that he had smoked too much pot the night before. He promised as soon as we arrived in Myrtle Beach, things would be different. Well, Myrtle Beach was no different.

For some ungodly reason, I wanted this union to work. I kept thinking of the statement my mother had said to me at the reception, "If this marriage does not work, I know it will be your fault." Actually, considering our history, this was probably a natural statement for her to make regarding me.

I had foolishly quit my perfect job, and was too proud to go back and admit to all the guys that my marriage lasted only through the wedding ceremony. Lou did not take the job in Richmond, and we lived with my mother for about a month before he secured a job in Pennsylvania.

The only reason this union was bearable was the fact that my best wedding present was a six-month-old American Eskimo Spitz. In my opinion, it is the most beautiful breed of any dog in the world. He was perfect in every way, and he loved me as much as I loved him.

The three of us moved to Pennsylvania, in what was referred to as, the worst winter in the United States. We arrived in a snowstorm and were stranded in a hotel for almost three months. Lou went to work on a snowmobile, and Efran and I stayed at the hotel, read, ate and watched the snow continue to fall. I did not see Lou much, and sometimes he was unable to get back to the hotel because of the snow, like I cared.

I had the maintenance people plow an area large enough for Efran to go out and do his business. I would watch him, but it was hard to see a solid white dog in solid white surroundings. I followed the yellow stream and I could always find him.

As I was eating, drinking and sitting most of the time, my weight started to climb. I am sure my depression had much to do with my weight gain. My old enemy was returning. I decided to call and make an appointment with a marriage counselor that day. The ice and snow had started to thaw. I informed Lou that we had an appointment the next week. On the scheduled day of the appointment, we visited the therapist and it was decided that we would need intensive therapy, and she scheduled weekly appointments.

During one of the sessions, Lou told the therapist that he had been impotent in his first two marriages. I told Susan, the therapist, that he was not impotent with himself. Lou said that he was intimidated by me because I carried a gun, and for this reason he was afraid of me. After I closed my mouth and gained my composure, I explained to Susan that my previous job was in law enforcement, and of course I carried a gun. I further informed Susan that while we were dating, Lou was actually impressed by the fact that I carried a gun. For some reason, Susan suggested that we find a church and see if attending a church would help us. We made another appointment for the following week.

I went back to the hotel and checked on Efran. I decided to ask some of the hotel staff about churches in the area. When you are snowbound at a hotel for three months, the staff quickly learns your name and your habits. I was told that the Unitarian Universalist Church was very prominent in the area. As I had never even heard of this church, I decided that we would go on Sunday. I loved the looks of the church, the people, the minister and the fact that children under the age of seven, were not allowed in the adult 10:30 AM service. The children had their service from 11:00 AM to 12:00 PM. During this half hour, the adults met for hors d'oeuvres and conversation. When the children's service was over, we could stay longer or not.

We attended church and joined a Sunday school class. I transferred my membership from the church I had joined when I was twelve to this new church. As I am obsessive compulsive, I volunteered for everything. As this was a dog friendly church, Efran accompanied me every time I volunteered. Spiritually, I felt that I had found a home.

During one service the minister mentioned Efran. I was honored until I was told that there was a man in the Bible named Efran. I know Lou only liked this church because most of the members were scholars and college professors. Lou often envisioned himself a scholar, but Efran and I knew different.

Lou and I became almost civil to each other. He and I would take Efran and go for day trips. As we lived in Amish country, we saw the lushest countryside. In all the neighboring towns and in front of every business establishment, posts were cemented in order for the Amish to tie their horses. The horse always had the right of way. The Amish are gifted farmers, woodworkers and building furniture. We were also introduced to the Mennonites; they were much more progressive than their Amish cousins. They actually drove black cars, and even the chrome was painted black.

One day, Lou called me and said that his company was closing the Pennsylvania site, and building an office in the town in which I grew up and that my mother still lived in. I was really stunned. He asked if I wanted to move and I decided to let his company pay for the shipping of my furniture. I knew that I would miss my church, but the minister gave me the names and addresses of several churches near my "new/old" home.

Lou flew to North Carolina, and Efran and I drove and took our time. I stopped to visit Maddy outside of Washington. She had married a guy from Hilton Head, and they were both in law school in D.C. We stayed about two days and then stopped to visit Martha in Raleigh, NC. She had married Tony, and he was working at the Research Triangle Park as an engineer. As they had two young children and a small apartment, Efran and I stayed at a nearby hotel. I then traveled to Winston-Salem to visit Ginger and Slick who now had three children. When Amy, their middle child was born, I was asked to be her godmother. This was such an honor and I appreciated them choosing me. Amy is such a beautiful child, with blond hair and blue eyes which she inherited from her parents. Her quick wit and intelligence she inherited from me, or so I liked to tell everyone. I enjoyed visiting with my friends, and we talked about old times, the fun we always had together and the fact that I would be close enough to visit on a regular basis. By the time I arrived at my new home, Lou had the furniture unpacked and everything put away. This was not exactly as I had planned, but I was too tired to argue.

The following week, I was contacted by a local college and asked to teach a criminal justice course to upperclassmen. I met with the department head the following week, and began teaching the course three days per week. I knew that I did not have the temperament to teach or the dedication to plan classes, but I knew I needed to get out of the house. Due to the church affiliation of the college, most students came from New Jersey. After teaching for about a month, I knew this profession was not for me. I also knew I had no intention of getting my masters.

As I still had contact in law enforcement, I decided to contact some agencies and offered to work on a contract basis. I was beginning to get my weight under control, for yet another time.

I knew I needed to see a therapist about dealing with Daddy's death. First, I had to get out of my loveless and destructive marriage. I left Lou, packed my furniture, put it in storage, and Efran and I moved in with my mother until I could begin working some assignments. My mother had always told me, "Never marry beneath you." A better statement is probably, "You can't make chicken salad out of chicken shit."

I found a therapist who concentrated in treating people who had lost loved ones. Through the sessions and my own perseverance, I finally accepted his death. It was as if a weight had been lifted off my shoulders and my heart.

Chapter 5

My Next Step Toward Freedom

Within the next six months, I met a man whose company I really enjoyed. Naturally, Lance was much older than I, and neither of us wanted nor expected anything but an uncomplicated relationship. We had fun together, traveled together and sometimes I was his co-pilot. He had never joined the mile high club, so I initiated him as a member.

He was about as far removed from my generation than anyone could be. Half the time when we talked about our lives, he did not understand what I was talking about. He taught me to ballroom dance, and I actually enjoyed it. He said that he admired my independence, my free spirit and my spunk.

He was not too old that he had not heard of beach music and the shag. When I mentioned the sixties and talked about the great times, he just listened. I told him that I had seen the production of "Hair," where at the end all the actors were nude. He started paying attention. When I discussed my conspiracy theories about almost everything, he thought I was nuts and stopped paying attention.

We spent New Year's Ever together in one of his many furniture stores. I was much more adventurous sexually that he, and I was determined to have sex on every mattress and chair in the store—and he was always game for everything. I told him that I have always heard that at midnight on New Year's Eve, a person should be doing what they want to do for the rest of the year. As the clock struck midnight, we were doing what we wanted to be doing for the rest of the year and longer.

In about two weeks, I started getting sick at my stomach, and just knew that I was pregnant. I fainted at work and was weak all the time. I took some time off from work to rest and had a pregnancy test. When it came back positive, I was not surprised.

What surprised me was the fact that I considered having a child. Lance and I cared for each other, and if I could have picked the perfect man to father my child, he would have been that man. He was intelligent, athletic, handsome, humorous, considerate and extremely successful. His children were grown: one had graduated from West Point, another from Harvard Law and the youngest was in her third year at Carolina. As he had contributed half of their excellent genes, I knew that our child would be almost perfect.

I visited Lance's closest friend, Mack, and discussed the situation with him. I explained to Mack that I had been weak and sick since the second week of the pregnancy, and that I had to make a decision quickly. I knew Mack would never tell Lance anything because I was his patient, and he was my doctor.

He had recently opened a birthing center and also performed abortions. As abortions were now legal in most states, Mack could perform the abortion if that was to be my choice. I thought about my decision and what I was going to do. I decided on an abortion. Seven weeks after the abortion, I had my tubes tied. Mack told me that while he was performing my tubal ligation, he noticed that I had some other problems.

In another month, I had my right ovary removed and it was discovered that I could never have carried a child full term. The ovary he removed was badly diseased, as were several other organs. He told me I had the worst case of endometriosis he had ever seen. Mack said he had removed all that he could, but could not understand why I had not been in severe pain for at least a year. I realized with this information, I had made the only decision I could have.

Lance could not understand why I was being so evasive, and I explained to him that my job had taken me out of town more than usual. He asked me if I had ever thought about us moving in together. I used the lame excuse that my divorce was not final and that I still had my career. When I returned to work, we slowly drifted apart.

After a couple more years of catching the bad guys, I decided to hand in my badge. I could remember when I never saw another female agent, whether in court or during raids. But times were changing, and more and more females were entering the field. I could only hope that they would have as great of an experience as I did.

Most law enforcement agents, even after serving many more years than I, have never had a shot fired at them, had guns pointed at them, fired their gun in the line of duty or testified, on a regular basis, in federal or state court as much as I had.

I left with my reputation in tact, and with a record of never having lost a case in court. Most importantly, I had gained the respect of everyone I worked with.

Chapter 6

Changes Are Good or Are They?

I decided to take a job in Charlotte working for the state again. The title of the job sounded as if I was still a sworn officer, but in reality nothing could have been further from the truth. This agency represented the custodial parent of children on welfare, to establish paternity and place the non-custodial parent on order to pay child support. The reason for this action was to help reimburse the state for welfare money. It was really a joke.

My friend "DD" was an agent at the agency. She and I had become close friends after "rookie school," and remained so through the years. "DD" had been offered a job before I was married with the Federal Witness Protection Agency. As the job required so much traveling, she was unable to take it. Her children, John and Missy, were still young and needed her supervision.

"DD" introduced me to the other agents and I really liked the ones I met. She also introduced me to several lawyers in the building beside ours, and I knew immediately that these men would be my buddies. One girl in my new office, Devi, and I became immediate friends.

This agency was like no other I had ever seen. The administration in the local office was, as I deemed it, "totally non discriminatory in their discrimination." This agency (with approximately 400 employees) had more grievances filed than one of the other state agencies that employed more than 10,000 employees. The office was like a powder keg waiting to explode. I was not accustomed to inept supervisors and ones that were ill trained and uneducated.

I understood having political friends. This was my second political appointment in state government. There are probably more political appointments than regular hires. There are two kinds of political appointments: the people who give big donations, that are given a job as head of an agency with a salary of $150K a year, and the people given peon jobs with a salary of about $23K a year. Unfortunately, I fell in this category.

If it had not been for my fellow workers and the guys next door, I would have quit. This was the kind of work environment where the supervisors and the director were never satisfied unless the office was in complete chaos. I tried to stay out of the inner office politics, but it was difficult. Many of the other agents looked to me for guidance and problem solving.

My work hours were great. I met friends every morning at the coffee shop next door, and every afternoon and into the night I partied with the attorneys in the building next door. I would drive home at about 4 AM, shower and be back for coffee by 7 AM. I had always "burned the candle at both ends" and still considered myself invincible. I still thought the lyrics of the Tam's song "Be Young, Be Foolish, Be Happy" were written for me. I had also read a book one night, while staying in some hotel in some city, that contained the phrase, "Live Fast, Die Young and Have a Good Looking Corpse." I always knew this was the way I would leave this world. With my lifestyle, there was really no other option. I knew that I would not live past fifty; therefore, I had to make the most of the next twelve or so years.

On May 8th, at 11 PM on a rainy night, my life changed. Debbie, my designated driver, and I decided to go to a hotel lounge and hear Bill Joe Royal. She had never heard of Billy Joe Royal, but I had. She was younger that I so I named some of his hits: *Down in the Boondocks, Cherry Hill Park,* and *I Knew You When.* She then said that she had heard of the songs but did not know he was the singer. When we entered the lounge, I noticed a life sized cardboard figure of a man that had to be Billy Joe, but he looked so pale and frail.

We found the table with the best view. I ordered a drink and ordered Debbie a wine, which she never intended to drink. We lit a cigarette and talked for a bit while waiting for Royal.

After drinking several more drinks, a hand reached around the table and used my ashtray to extinguish his cigarette. The thing that really made me mad was the fact that he didn't even bother to crush it out. As he was attempting small talk, I moved the ashtray out of my way. He asked if he could sit down and I motioned him to do so. He was a sickly looking guy, and I felt that he needed to sit down before he fell down.

He asked if either of us had ever seen Billy Joe Royal. I said that I had seen him in the late sixties, and had actually donated a pint of blood for a ticket to his performance. He asked what I thought of the performance, and I said that it was great and he was so cute. I then stated, looking at the cardboard figure, I could not believe how much he had aged and wondered if he were gay. About the same time, the drums rolled and the MC announced Billy Joe Royal. The person at our table stood up and went on stage. As I was sitting there with my foot in my mouth, he started to sing and his voice was still the same. I will give Billy Joe this much, he gave a great performance and didn't seem to be affected by my comment.

Debbie wanted to leave before the show was over. I told her that the damage was done, and even if I apologized to him, what would I say? Perhaps something to the effect, "I did not mean gay. I meant happy?" As we were staying at a hotel about thirty minutes away, we decided to leave about fifteen minutes early.

The valet brought my car around and I got in the passenger side. As it was drizzling, she was driving pretty slowly. We drove for about thirty minutes. As she was making a turn, she threw her cigarette out the window and it blew back in the car and landed on the back seat. As I was turning around to retrieve it, she ran straight into a telephone pole. We hit dead on, and the hood of my brand new car was split in half. She had her seatbelt on, but I did not. By law, a passenger did not have to wear one.

My head hit the windshield with enough force to crack it. My body was thrown back in the seat, and then I was thrown toward the floorboard legs first. As the car was so damaged by the telephone pole, my left foot went through the floorboard. Of course, this all happened in the flash of a moment. By the time I pushed my body out of the car and onto the grass, I was completely sober.

Luckily, the EMS was directly behind us and immediately transported me to the hospital. As my injuries were much for severe, I was taken in the first ambulance. Another had been called for Debbie, who had been protected by her seatbelt. Debbie probably did not weigh over ninety pounds, and I always felt this protected her from serious injury.

There were three hospitals in Charlotte, and I chose the wrong one. All passengers and drivers in this type of accident were given blood tests to determine alcohol content. Mine went through the ceiling. As this was a moot issue because I was not the driver, I was not concerned. I did hear some comment about how in the world could this girl carry on a completely sober conversation and register so high on the blood alcohol content scale. I have always been able to hold my liquor, but the accident had helped me to sober up.

I was trying to tell the doctors what to do. Naturally, they were not listening, so I started talking louder and demanding more. A cop came over and asked me to be quiet. I spoke some expletives and told him to please find me a real doctor. He left to find somebody if for no other reason, than to shut me up.

The doctors were more concerned about my head injury than anything else. I had probably suffered at least six serious head injuries since I was two, and I did not think that this injury was anything to be alarmed about. Health professionals think they know everything, and that the patient does not know anything.

I had the hospital call "DD," and she came to the hospital with three attorney friends. Two of them were the ones I partied with most night. I told "DD" not to call my mother, but she had already called her.

I was in a treatment room waiting for an orthopedist to come while about three residents were pouring water over my forehead trying to wash glass off. I asked for a particular orthopedic firm to be called.

I could hear my mother in the hall as she was approaching. When she entered, she was accompanied by my uncle, my father's only brother. As they were standing there a doctor came in. He seemed to know my uncle, and they talked about golf and their upcoming golf match the following week. I am so glad they had that time together. My uncle and mother left until his examination was completed.

The doctor finally came over to talk to me and explained that most of my injuries were confined to my left side: my heel was crushed, my ankle was broken and my toes were all broken. He explained to me that my ankle needed to be set and I needed to have surgery. I told him if I needed surgery, I would use a family friend who was an orthopedist in my hometown.

The bastard decided to set my ankle right then and there, and without telling me what he was about to do. The pain was terrible, but it did not take me but a second to retaliate. I took my good foot and kicked him as hard as I could across the room into a cabinet. One thing for sure, he didn't play golf the next week. I had to spend the night at the hospital in Charlotte and was transported to my doctor's office the following morning. I had surgery within three hours.

When I returned to work six weeks later, I only worked four hours per day and had physical therapy for two hours. One of my closest friends at the office insisted that I move in with her. I moved a single bed into her extra bedroom, and stayed with her for about two months. I also brought a stereo and my records. Thank God she loved beach music also.

As I thought more about my physical condition, or lack thereof, I became extremely concerned about my sexual activities, and would I be able to have sex again. The physical therapist gave me a book about sexual positions for people with disabilities. The book even had pictures of different positions. Then it dawned on me, what about my other pastime, dancing? Would I ever be able to shag again? I could not believe that I was in this predicament.

The insurance company did not total the car for six months. As it was totaled the night of the accident, I decided to speak with one on my attorney coffee buddies. He advised me to call the company again and tell them I would be renting a car until they decide what to do. When I told them that, they immediately decided to total my car. Now I had their attention and decided to add a few demands of my own. I told the adjustor that I also wanted to be reimbursed for the six months of lease payments and insurance premiums I had made. They also agreed to that.

I was getting along well with the physical therapy and nothing major could be done at present. My doctor and all the specialists had told me that I would have to wait for at least ten years, or until I was in a wheelchair, to have the hip and knee replacements. I knew I had to get on with life.

Chapter 7

Was I Ready to Settle Down?

I decided to rent a house with a fenced in yard so Efran could come and live with me. My mother had a fit. She said that he needed someone with him all the time, and that he needed freedom, not a fenced in yard. She had decided that since she had been keeping him for me, that he needed to stay at her house. She still had Yohann, but she loved Efran also. I explained to her that I was Efran's mother and that I would decide what was best for him.

I searched for a house with a fenced in yard, but could not find one in a neighborhood I liked. I found one I liked, but the owner would not let me put a fence up. I told him that I would buy the damn house, but he didn't want to sell it so I rented it.

Every weekend I picked up Efran and took him to the parks and for rides. He hated the fact that he had to wear a collar and be lead around on a leash. I was not going to have the same thing happen to him as had happened to Snoopy.

I entertained every weekend as the layout of the house was made for entertaining. There was an oriental courtyard surrounded by a wall that separated the two wings. I had to hire a gardener to clean it up and plant what needed to be planted. After it was completed, I had the look of a garden in Japan. I also had a green house, but decided that I did not want any of that. I have always been basically lazy, and did not want to even be bothered with anything that I would have to keep up. I did wire the inside and outside of the house with a sound system and bought a jukebox.

About a month after having my wreck, Debbie had introduced me to her brother-in-law. He was a nice guy and we double dated with Debbie and her husband. Debbie had recovered from the accident and walked out of it with only a couple of bruises.

Robert, the brother-in-law, could have passed for Kenny Rogers. He traveled on a regular basis and I did not see him that much. I had a lot going on in my life and did not need any added complications.

There seemed to be people at my house all the time. I contacted JB and some of my law enforcement friends. Most were no longer with the state and JB was sticking around until retirement. He, his family and others came for barbeques, and all my male friends knew that they were responsible for all the grilling. I furnished the music, the alcoholic beverages and the food. I guess that was the reason I had so many visitors. Whatever the reason, everyone had a great time and so did I.

In December, I decided to have a Christmas party and this started a tradition. One thing I do, is entertain and entertain well. There were about seventy people at the first party. As I had plenty of room, anyone who felt they could not drive spent the night. Many of my friends from out of town came and stayed in local hotels: Liz, Ginger and Slick, Robin and Chuck, Chandelier, Martha and Tony and others. My "coffee group," Mary Ellen, Judy and Charles, Bill, Keith, Mike and Amon were there in full swing. I also invited my mother and told her to bring any friends she wished to bring.

I made eggnog, one with brandy and one plain. I was hoping that everyone would finish all of it, and luckily they did. As I could drink a gallon of my eggnog, I did not want any left as a temptation. One of the guys in my office had a catering business, so I planned the menu and he cooked, served and cleaned up afterwards. Efran and Yohann were dressed to impress in a tux and evening dress. That lasted about five minutes. From then on they went "natural."

At around midnight, my doorbell rang and one of the guests answered it. When I looked around, Robert was standing in the living room. As I did not remember inviting him, I was surprised to see him there. I told him to get a plate and help himself. He asked me if he could talk to me, and I explained that this was not a good time. He walked into the dining room and introduced himself to my guests. Everybody asked if he was related to Kenny Rogers. He said that he was not, but that he still had a home in Tennessee, up the mountain from where Willie Nelson had once lived. Even I stopped what I was doing and listened. (Beach music was not the only music I enjoyed.)

My mother, her friends and my sister left the following afternoon, and I called Robert and invited him over. He told me that he loved me and had since the first time he met me. As I am not totally naïve, I knew that no one could fall in love on the first date. He then proceeded to give me a gold necklace with matching gold earrings. They were beautiful and I was surprised that he had ever heard of Tiffany's. He asked if he could take me out the following weekend. As the next week was Christmas and I had other commitments, I declined. When he asked about New Year's, I accepted.

I spent Christmas Eve and Christmas night with my mother, Efran and Yohann. As I am a child at heart, Christmas has always been my favorite time of the year. I love the music, the decorations, the cakes and pies, the festive atmosphere, the exchanging of gifts and the smell of the Christmas tree. All of my great feelings of Christmas come from the days when I was a child. My parents made this time of the year the greatest ever, and I believed in Santa Clause until I was almost thirteen.

All families had rituals and ours were probably no different from anybody else's. We put cookies and milk out on Christmas Eve and went to bed early. (Of course, I am sure we never slept much.) Before we could go downstairs, we had to call down and ask, "Has Santa Clause come yet?" Mother and Daddy would have to go into the living room to check and see before they would answer. After they checked and told us that Santa had come, we would run down the stairs. Our stockings, with our names on them, would be full and placed on the two wing back chairs. Around each chair, Santa had placed our presents. After we looked at these gifts, Daddy would sit on the floor and give out the presents from under the tree. If Wills or his sister had not called us, we would call them and eagerly tell each other what Santa had brought us.

After we ate our usual breakfast of pancakes and link sausages, we always had to go to our Daddy's parents' home. My grandmother was a wonderful cook, and I would head straight for the dining room to check out the pies and cakes. My grandfather was always so much fun, and my memories of him are still fresh in my mind. My Daddy's two sisters and their families would already be at our grandparents' house. We would exchange gifts and then go outside until we were called in for the typical Christmas meal. Later in the day, we would travel back home and finally get to play with our gifts again. This was repeated every Christmas for years. After my father died, Christmas, nor anything, else was ever the same again.

As I had gotten older, Mother had developed a habit of giving me money, with the excuse, "You are just so particular and hard to please." I finally told her that next year, even if I had to return my gifts, she needed to put forth an effort.

I had had enough disappointment so I left about eleven to visit my aunt. She and I have always been close. As she has sons, we almost had a mother/daughter relationship. She is very important to me and taught me many things. Two pieces of advice, which I will never forget, are, "Presentation is the key." And "If you need to ask the price, you don't need it." We both liked to smoke and have our drinks and today was no different. I stayed and visited for about two hours and drove back to my mother's to pick up Efran.

On the way back to my house, Efran and I stopped at "DD's" to see what Santa had brought Missy and Johnny. Their house was full of excitement and empty packages were everywhere. We exchanged gifts and I drove to my house.

In a couple of days, Robert called to see how I was doing and to wish me a Merry Christmas. He asked me if I would like to spend New Years in Nashville with his business partner and his wife. I told him that we would need to fly because I had to be back at work the day after New Years. He said that he would make the arrangements and pick me up the night before New Year's Eve. I knew that Nashville was known as the country music capital of the world; therefore, I decided to buy an outfit that really sparkled with a western flair. I also decided to take my tuxedo, pants suits and my jeans.

As I was unable to wear heels any longer, I bought a pair of dress shoes with a thin heel that was about a half inch high. (big mistake) While I was shopping, I bought Robert a Stetson hat for the upcoming trip. I have never allowed anyone to give me anything without doing something in return. I took Efran back to my mother's and then returned home to pack.

Robert picked me up about 7:00 PM and we left for the airport. When we passed the Charlotte Airport, I realized we were going to a private airstrip. When we got there I was introduced to his business partner and his wife. They were nice, but not really my kind of people.

At about the same time, his partner asked me if I wanted to co-pilot. I noticed a Lear parked alone on the airstrip. I said that I was not certified to fly a jet. Actually, it had been awhile since I had even flown any type of plane. As it turned out, there were two pilots ready to take us to Nashville. Evidently, Robert had told his partner that I had my license, but I know they were playing a joke on me. No owner of a Lear or any privately owned plane, would allow a stranger to get behind the controls of his plane.

As we arrived in Nashville about the same time we left Charlotte, due to the one-hour time difference, the flight was quick and nice. I had never been to Nashville, but evidently everyone on the flight was a regular. Robert told me that we were booked at the Hermitage Hotel in downtown Nashville. I asked him if the hotel were named after the home of Andrew Jackson. He said that Andrew Jackson's home was a historical site located near where we were staying.

My godmother was a Jackson and was his descendant. If you were to place a $20 bill beside seven of her twelve children, you would think you were looking at the same person. I decided to visit the Jackson Museum while in Nashville and then remembered that it would be closed for the holiday. Oh well, I would visit it the next trip.

Nashville is a beautiful city, and everywhere you go you are reminded of country music in a good way. The only country artists I was familiar with were The Outlaws, Kris Kristofferson, Johnny Cash, Dolly Parton, Glen Campbell, Johnny Cash and some of the old timers. As Robert and his friends were very familiar with all of the artists, they got tickets for Kenny Rogers and Johnny Cash. They threatened to take me to a club downtown that featured bluegrass music, and I told them that we would go down that road the next trip.

The lobby of The Hermitage Hotel was elegant and still decorated for Christmas. Everywhere you looked was a winter wonderland. I was surprised that three rooms would be available so close to New Year's Eve.

Our rooms were large, and after I got settled, I headed for the lounge. I had noticed the lounge when we entered and also heard heavy hors d'oeuvres calling my name. The lounge was rockin' with the sound of country music and I settled in with my drink and goodies. After about thirty minutes, my traveling companions joined me. We made small talk and I asked the guy what kind of business he was in. He said he was in the trucking business, and that he owned a racing team. I was surprised that he didn't own a Gulfstream. He quickly told me that he and Robert were involved in other business ventures. I decided to stop asking questions.

I wore my western garb when we went out that night, but I could have worn jeans. Robert was really a gentleman, which I appreciated. He and I walked down Broadway and could hear music everywhere. The city was very festive and Christmas decorations were everywhere.

We met our companions and attended the concerts. Both Kenny and Johnny were great and I enjoyed hearing them both. I did notice Kenny looking at Robert and was surprised that he did not come over. They really did favor each other. At midnight we wore the customary crazy hats, and blew the blowouts and horns. Everybody hugged and kissed and acted silly and crazy. (which is right down my alley) At 12:01 AM on New Years, everybody is happy and hugs and kisses anybody they see. This was my kind of way to celebrate, but after thirty minutes I noticed I did not see Robert or my traveling companions. The celebration must have been too much excitement for them.

I decided to walk back to the hotel, but after about ten minutes I had to toss my shoes in the nearest trash bin. The new shoes were killing my feet, and I decided that walking barefoot would be more comfortable. I went to the nearest club, sat down and ordered a drink. After consuming about six drinks, Robert and his companions came in. As I was sitting in a corner with some guy who had decided that I need company, I waited until my "friends" looked around and walked out. Robert looked nervous and upset. All I thought was that they should not have walked out on the party and on me.

In about thirty minutes I left, found a cab and went back to the hotel. The doorman looked at my bare feet, stopped me and asked my room number. Of course, I didn't remember my room number, but I did remember the floor number. He still looked suspicious and asked me my name. Before I could say Robert's last name, I felt a hand on my shoulder. I turned quickly and looked up and saw Robert's face. The doorman did not ask me anything further. Robert and I walked to the elevator and he escorted me to my room. As he had my key, he opened the door for me.

Once inside, he said that he was worried to death, was sorry that we had become separated and continued to apologize for the next few minutes. I told him that I was a big girl, had taken care of myself for years and would continue to do so. He then proceeded to tell me that he wanted to take care of me for the rest of my life, and wanted me to move into his house with him. I explained to him that he must have had too much champagne, but I did appreciate his concern.

Before he could answer, I suggested that we go to the lounge, listen to the music and have some fun. After all, we had just entered a new year and I had come to Nashville for an uncomplicated holiday. As we were scheduled to return to Charlotte at about 7:00 PM, I wanted to make the best of the remainder of our time.

I did not see Robert's business partner or his wife until we boarded the plane. Our trip back was uneventful. Robert drove me home, and I explained to him that I had to get some sleep before I returned to work in less than eight hours. After he left, I turned on my jukebox and listened to my beach music for the remainder of the night.

I still visited my attorney friends in the building next door for our usual afternoon cocktails, but I no longer stayed all night. These guys were the greatest men in the world. Most were old time lawyers who had represented the owners of the first topless clubs in Charlotte, and had made their money many years ago. Many times some friends from my office would venture in and out. Even "DD" would stop by for a drink once in a while. I never invited Robert.

Robert stopped by my office one day and many of my co-workers thought he was Kenny Rogers. Robert could be very charming in many ways. Most of my friends, both male and female, liked him.

We started dating in the way that I would describe as courting. As I always heard this phrase in the westerns, it seemed to me that this was the most accurate description. He was polite, generous and gracious. I had previously told him to stop talking about his undying love for me, and evidently he decided to do so.

I knew he wanted more from me than I wanted from him. I was still apprehensive about starting a sexual relationship due to my physical disabilities. I told him as much, but naturally he said that he would wait. He asked if he could borrow my book on sex and disabilities.

I did notice that he did not travel as often as he did when I first met him. The poor man had no taste in clothes and had never cared about what he wore. I told him that I needed to take him shopping for clothes. As he agreed with just about everything I said, we proceeded to go shopping. He had to shop at the big and tall stores. I don't think he even knew the cost of nice clothes or had even been to an upscale clothier.

Although he needed to shop at the big and tall stores, it was obvious he never had. A salesman approached us and I proceeded to tell him what we needed. When the salesman proceeded to measure him, I could tell Robert was uncomfortable.

The salesman showed him several pairs of slacks, sport jackets, knit shirts and dress shirts. I found a seat and waited until he tried on each item and walked out to show it to me. At least everything fit him properly for once. A couple pair of pants needed to be hemmed. When the tailor came out, I suggested he cuff the pants. When the tailor started to measure, Robert turned red as a beet. I guess he was embarrassed to have another man be so close. I almost burst out laughing.

As my aunt had always told me, "If you have to ask the price, you don't need to buy it." No one had told Robert that. Since Robert had always bought cheaper clothes that did not fit, he was never concerned about the price. He had never seen a pair of slacks for $200, but knew by my expression that he was going to buy whatever I said. He and I walked out of the store and his wallet was much thinner. I knew that he paid only with cash, as he didn't believe in credit cards.

That night when we went out, he looked very good and much more like Kenny Rogers. I bought him his first pair of Weejuns and dark socks. (up to his mid calf) He would never have worn shoes without socks. Even I could not talk him into that. As we were walking out the car, and as he was opening the door for me, I just happened to glance down and saw that he had on white tube socks. I yelled at him and pointed at his feet. He looked down and said that he had forgotten to put his dark socks on. I told him that if he wanted to go out that night with me, we would have to stop by his house to pick up the other socks. He grumbled something about reservations but we sped to his house.

During our meal, he asked me if I were even interested in him. I told him that he certainly was more presentable, but I would never have sex with anyone again if that person did not have an AIDS test and show me the results. As someone in the health care field had told me, a person needed to have the test done twice, one test one month and the second in the next thirty days.

Every female knows the next statement from a male. Something like, "I am particular whom I date and I wouldn't date someone who would have diseases." Maybe they had not heard the old saying; "A man would screw a snake if we wouldn't be afraid of it biting his dick off." Anyway, he said that he would have the two tests and show me the results. Well, I put any other conversation regarding sex on hold for sixty days.

I did vent to Robert about the job, and it was nice to have some objective person to talk with. He told me to quit and find something else, or let him take care of me. I did not even respond.

We still dated on a regular basis and we had a great time together. We traveled to Tennessee on several occasions. His grandchild lived in the home that Robert had built over fifteen years ago, with her mother, Robert's daughter, and her father. I knew Robert had been alienated from the rest of his family since he ran away when he was twelve. I really did not ask nor care what had happened with his ex-wife, his family or his daughter.

As in most divorces, the child chooses the mother. His daughter was no different, though she did call him when the child was born. This was mainly because she needed financial help and Robert was the parent who could provide it. I realize that parents are forgiving, especially fathers with daughters. The baby looked just like her mother, and I thought to myself, "poor child."

We flew to Vegas and saw some shows. I realized that Tom Jones and Wayne Newton looked almost the same as they did the last time I saw them, except with wrinkles. We had just missed three of the "Rat Pack," Sinatra, Dean Martin and Sammy Davis, Jr. I really hated that, but decided I would get tickets to see them the next time they were in Vegas.

Robert said that he had a business meeting, and I told him that I wanted to go back to the Hoover Dam and Lade Mead again. I thought about going on to Los Angeles and seeing some of the sights that I wanted to see. I still loved movies and had never lost my attraction for California or anything to do with the entertainment industry. As Robert was to be occupied for at least a day, I decided to take a helicopter ride over the Grand Canyon instead of flying on to Los Angeles.

If I had been determined and not so lazy, I would have gotten my license to fly a helicopter. The instruments in a helicopter are much more complicated than in any type of airplane I have ever flown or flown in. Being a passenger in one is still a lot of fun. I had a great time and took a couple of rolls of film. This was the first time I had been in something this cramped since my accident. It was worth it.

Robert was outside of the casino when I drove up. He waved and the men he was with turned and went back inside the casino. We toured the city that night, and the lights and activity were just as it was the last time I was here. I was beginning to enjoy his company more and more.

Robert had always been secretive about his profession, but it would have taken a complete idiot not to figure it out. I guess this was to be the third time I had become involved with someone with connections to the Mafia. Robert's job had to be different from my other two friends because Robert was not Italian or Catholic. It was no use quizzing him. I just let it slide.

Months went by and finally Robert showed me the results of his two AIDS tests. He was clean. He just smiled and indicated to me what he hoped was to happen now. I just looked at him and started another conversation, but in the back of my mind I was considering the situation.

About six weeks later, he sold his house and moved in with me. He knew that I did not cook, clean or pick up after anyone but Efran and myself. Robert had lived alone for a long time and did not have any trouble taking care of his personal needs. He was just as kind, thoughtful and generous as he was when I first met him. He never failed to bring me a present when he returned home from his trips, and always insisted that we reserve each weekend for something special. Our life together was enjoyable and exciting.

After Christmas, he was on a trip out west and was in a horrible accident. When I was contacted, his business partner had someone fly me to New Mexico. The town was really a reservation and the hospital was not the best. Due to his condition, he was transported to Albuquerque and I followed the ambulance. The highway was one of the worst I had ever driven on. About every mile or so, I had to swerve to miss the potholes in the highway. As I was driving and trying to miss potholes, I noticed the ambulance swerving and I hoped that Robert was totally knocked out with morphine. While in Albuquerque, Robert had several orthopedic procedures. Some were life threatening, but he made it through.

I am not a hospital person, and I do not believe in staying in the room while someone sleeps all the time. I am too hyperactive for that. I was there for all the procedures and talked with his doctors. My feelings have always been if you are sick enough to be in the hospital, you are sick enough not to have visitors.

I spent the majority of my time riding around the city, reading and relaxing in the hotel spa. I really loved Albuquerque, but not the hot spicy food. I had tasted Mexican food, but not **real** Mexican food. I really don't like either.

When Robert was ready to be transferred to a rehabilitation hospital, I decided to leave. I called his partner and he sent his plane for me that same day. That next morning, after staying six weeks, I flew back to Charlotte.

His partner met me at the landing strip and told me that I did not have to worry about anything financially. As I had found Robert's "bag money," I knew I did not have to worry about anything financial for a long time. I returned to work on Monday. Everyone seemed glad to see me. Of course, no one had done anything with my stack of paperwork.

Robert was transferred to Charlotte Orthopedic Hospital where he stayed for about four weeks. When he returned home, he was given round the clock nurses. Thank God, I knew that I could not take on that responsibility.

That night, his parents came to my house to visit. Not only had I never seen his parents, I did not know Robert even had any contact with either of them. After about an hour, several other family members came to my house. I was getting pissed. I was civil and asked very politely how they knew where I lived. They answered that Robert had called them while at Charlotte Rehab and asked them to come by. Now, I was livid.

I am a private person and am particular about who comes in my home. Now, here is this family of vagabonds, who are not my invited guests, and the children are playing with my valuables. The children's manners, or lack of them, were only surpassed by those of their parents.

By listening to the conversation, I learned that they had been living in Charlotte for many years, and had been in contact with Robert, AKA Bobby. This did not sound anything like Robert had told me.

His mother was fussing and making over Bobby like he was five years old. I was almost sick to my stomach. I could not take it anymore, and excused myself and went into my bedroom, locked the door and immediately called "DD" to vent.

I got up the next morning and prepared to go to work. As I was walking toward the kitchen, I noticed that his mother was cooking breakfast and had her housecoat on. This meant that she had spent the night in Bobby's room to take care of him. I couldn't wait to leave, but I had to walk by her on the way out. She seemed shocked to see me and said hello. I asked her where the nurse was, and she said she could take better care of Bobby so she sent the nurse home. Well, I lost it! I told her that the nurses were under doctor's orders and that she was not to interfere any longer, and if she wanted to take care of Bobby at her house, she could take him there now. She started crying and attempted to apologize just as my back door opened and in walked Robert's father and brother. I looked shocked, and told them that they needed to knock before they entered my house. The father showed me a key that Bobby had given them and told them to come over any time. I asked for the key and he gave it to me.

I called work and explained that I would be in after lunch. I was not going to leave these people in my house alone. There was a knock on the door, and I walked by the brother to see who it was. It was the first shift nurse, and I was never so glad to see anybody in my life. She looked at me and asked if she was supposed to come and help take care of Robert or not. I answered her emphatically in the positive that she was to keep coming every day.

Robert's family looked hurt, but got their stuff together and walked out. I immediately marched into the spare bedroom and told Robert that the nurses would be taking care of him. He looked stunned, but didn't say anything. He was too busy telling me how bad he felt. He was not the kind of person that you could ever ask, "How are you feeling?" because he would tell you for an hour in detail. I decided to go to work before I exploded.

Robert was progressing each day, but the nurses stayed on, Thank God. On one occasion, the rehab supervisor came to visit me and to report on Robert's progress. After she was finished, I explained to her that Robert was suffering from some sort of brain trauma, and that this problem was much worse than his physical problems. She asked me to elaborate, which I did for the next two hours. She told me that she would request more records from Albuquerque and see if any head trauma was noticed.

When Robert could walk with a cane, I took him on long drives. As my car was a two-seater, we used the truck. He seemed almost sane during these trips. Most of the time at home, his behavior was erratic, to say the least.

One day he mentioned that he thought we should get a puppy. Well, this was fine with me. He had already looked in the paper and found some collie puppies for sale. I thought he was too old to even remember Lassie.

We went by and I found the cutest puppy I had seen in a long time. Naturally, I fell in love at first glance. The puppy was a Pomeranian, five weeks old, and I decided this was the puppy for me. I paid for my puppy, and told the breeder to hold him until the next day. After all, I had to purchase a baby pen and whatever else a baby would need.

As the Pomeranian is a spin off of the Spitz breed, I hoped Efran would love him as much as I did. Of course, I knew this would never happen. Robert loved the puppy also, and he never realized that this puppy was not a collie. His head injury must have been much worse than I thought. I went shopping at a baby (two-legged) store that same afternoon, and found what I thought I needed.

The next morning, I went back to the breeder and picked up my new baby boy. We named him Brokus because both Robert and I were physically broken up. To help Robert feel needed, I put both our names on the AKC papers. Of course, I paid for Brokus.

Brokus, Broke for short, did not stay in his pen with his clock long. I just could not stand it. I had to have him sleep with me. By this time Robert was also sleeping in the bed. Of course, all he did was complain about his health.

I went into the kitchen about four times until I brought him in the bedroom. I put him under the covers and by morning I could not find him. I looked over the side of the bed, and there he was no bigger than the palm of my hand, looking up at his mama with big brown eyes and asking me to pick him up. Of course, I did and he became my companion and my "son."

Anybody who does not love animals can never love anyone. With animals, I do definitely believe in love at first sight. I hated to even go to work each day. Fortunately, the first shift nurse was a true dog lover and played with Broke all day long. Robert played with Broke, but if the nurse had not been at the house I would have quit work and become a "full time mom."

Months passed, Broke grew to about seven pounds and was the smartest child anywhere. I do not want to slight Efran because I loved him dearly, and he was absolutely perfect. Efran was living with my mother, therefore I only saw him about twice a week.

My relationship with Robert was at a stand still, just as my job was. About ten of my fellow workers would meet every day before work and vent our hate for the job and supervisors. When people started talking about coming to work one day with an Uzi and killing all the people we hated, I decided it was time to find another job.

I also knew that my relationship with Robert was coming to and end. I was a little more apprehensive about leaving Robert than my job. Robert's mental health seemed to be getting worse each day. He had found a job with a friend of his and he was working every day, at his own pace. The job seemed to help him some, but not as much as it should have. He refused to see any mental health professional, as this was weak for a man to do. "Real men don't see shrinks," was his response. The nurse had checked on his medical records and found nothing unusual about his mental well being. I told her that she did not live with him and he was becoming totally irrational. He had told me that if I ever left, he would kill me and Broke. As he was not the only one who carried a gun in the household, and I was a much better shot, I was not really concerned about this. The situation with Broke bothered me more than anything.

I contacted a friend who worked in a very high level position within state government, and he found a job for me in about two weeks. I was offered several positions, but decided to accept one near my mother's house.

As I was still renting the house, I contacted the owner and told him of my plans. I paid the next month's rent in order for Robert to have a place to live. I called a good friend I had worked with at ALE and asked him to come be with me while the movers were packing, just in case Robert came home. I sat on the porch with my trusted Colt Woodsman, and he sat in a car across the street with his 9mm. It was just like old times. After the furniture was packed on the truck, the movers followed me to my storage building and unpacked for me.

I had arranged to move in with a friend for about two or three weeks. She lived about a mile from the main road and I parked in her garage. This did not deter Robert from driving down her private drive and looking around to try and find me. I decided to go ahead and move in with my mother, as my friend was getting a little nervous.

I had bought a new car that Robert had never seen. As Robert was driving by my mother's house and most of my friend's houses, they all went to the sheriff's department and attempted to take out a restraining order. Well, the county did not issue restraining orders anymore.

I was at my mother's on Sunday afternoon and noticed Robert was driving by her house. After Robert had driven by about thirty times, I decided enough was enough. I loaded my 12 gauge with double "00" shot and walked to the end of the drive. He was just sitting there and pointing his finger at me and stepping on the gas and brake at the same time. I told him he was trespassing, and to leave and never come back. He moved a little toward me, and I pointed the shotgun, shot out his headlights and reloaded. I could see he was a little stunned, but he backed up, threw gravel all over and spun off. As he was headed down the road, I could hear the sheriff's cars racing up the other road. He never came to any of my friend's, nor my mother's homes again.

Chapter 8

My Social Awareness of the Sixties
Began to Surface

The next week I started my new job. My supervisor was female, and was the best female I had ever worked for. I had complete freedom and was never bothered by her or anyone else. Of course, my statistics were over the top. I traveled four counties and usually was in my office about once every week or two weeks. I had an interesting caseload and I became as socially conscious as I was in the sixties.

I worked for a state agency that actually helped people with disabilities. The name of the agency was Vocational Rehabilitation. My caseload was strictly a Social Security caseload. Every client I had in my caseload was either on SSDI (Social Security Disability) or SSI. (Supplemental Social Security) As my budget was primarily funded by Social Security, the money was endless. My clients were great and appreciated everything that was done for them. This agency was a remarkable agency and did more good than any other agency of this type.

Most of my co-workers had only been out of college a couple of years. As I have always acted and looked much younger than my age, it took a long time for them to realize that I was at least fifteen years older. Actually, if the truth were told, I was old enough to be their mother. A young mother, but I still could have been their mother.

When people asked if I had any children, I told them two boys. Most could never see me settled enough to have children. Sometimes I would work on Saturday and take Efran and Broke to work with me. They were a big help.

After I was working about six months, I was served with a lawsuit. Robert was suing me for a number of stupid things. One was that he wanted Broke. Like hell. I contacted the lawyer who was handling my lawsuit against the insurance company regarding my automobile accident. He said that he would handle this case for me.

I completed the absurd inter-derogatory statement and mailed them to my lawyer. On the day of court, the courtroom was empty except for my lawyer and me and Robert and his parents. He was a grown man with his momma and daddy to protect him. Will wonders never cease!

The attorney Robert had hired had dropped the suit after about a month of filing the lawsuit. Even he thought it was the most stupid case he had ever seen. The judge was a past friend of mine, and I felt as though I should have stood up and told him that Robert was crazy and I was sorry to take up the court's time.

After about three hours of testimony, the judge announced he was ready to rule. He ruled in my favor and made the statement, "I have been on the bench for fifteen years, and I have never witnessed a case such as this. Not only are these two people not married, the main issue is the custody of a dog." When my attorney explained to him that when he finalized his written ruling, that he had to state Broke's full name in order for me to have Robert's name taken off the AKC papers, he just rolled his eyes. I found out that having a co-owner's name removed from the original AKC papers involves more legal procedures than adopting a two-legged child. When the proceedings were over, I knew Robert was out of my life forever.

I returned to work the following day and started sifting through the dozens of applications from social security to review for potential clients. As I covered four counties, I was never without new clients.

Many of the people that I chose to interview did not become clients. They were just too disabled physically and mentally. I once interviewed three siblings from the same family whose IQ's together only totaled 50. Needless to say, they did not become my clients.

The goal of this agency was to find a job for the clients. Most had to be trained to either enter or reenter the workforce. I sent the majority of my clients to local technical schools or to Goodwill Industries for training. As all of my clients were indigent, they received financial aid from the colleges, but State VR picked up the bulk of the bills. In my case, Social

Security reimbursed State VR for all of my clients placed successfully in jobs. My success rate was about 96%.

One day my mother called and told me that she thought Efran was sick. She had taken him to the hospital, and it was discovered that he had cancer. I left work and stopped by the vet's office. We had taken our dogs to this vet since he opened his doors in 1970. He explained to me that he would start chemo the next day, but Efran's condition was terminal. I left his office devastated but glad that I had Broke. I am the type of person who could not live without a dog. Every animal I had ever had I, though of as my child. Where else can a person find total and complete unconditional love than from a dog?

After the chemo treatment Efran acted as though he were a puppy. I took him to the places he had always enjoyed the most. After three glorious months he came over to me, placed his head on my lap and just looked at me. It was as if he were saying that he could not hold on any longer. That night he died and a part of me did also.

As several of my friends had been keeping up wit Efran and his condition, I called to inform them of the bad news. Several immediately came over, and one of my male friends prepared Efran for burial in the lot beside my mother's house. This lot was now known as "our pet cemetery." He was buried near Snoopy's plot.

My family had just been reduced to two instead of three. Thank God I still had Broke and that he was still young. I called my supervisor that night and told her what had happened, and she said that she would cover my appointments.

I really enjoyed my job with State VR, but I realized that I had to increase my salary. I had never experienced the feeling of changing people's lives for the better, and it actually made me feel good. Now it was time for me to feel good.

I was not getting any younger and my love and demand for the finer things in life could not be met on a state employee's salary. Of course, there were few jobs that could meet my desires. I was talking to some fellow counselors, and they informed me that after being a VR counselor for a couple of years, most people entered the private rehabilitation field. When I heard them say that the salary was unbelievable, I immediately found the names of the best-known private rehab companies in the county and submitted my resumes.

After interviewing with several companies, I found one company that appeared to be a perfect fit for me. Margaret, the director of the vocational department that was located outside of Washington, met me in Charlotte, NC. After talking with me for about an hour, she offered me a position.

As salary was my main concern, she explained to me that this was entirely up to me. As I was being hired as a self-employed contractor, my salary was dependant on my abilities. She explained to me that she could tell by talking with me that I possessed the perfect combination of determination and innate traits needed to succeed in this job. I realized that I would be in a position to make any salary I wanted.

I explained to her that I had just been informed by my supervisor at VR that I had been nominated, and was chosen, as counselor of the year. I told her that I felt I should wait until after the award ceremony to begin working with her. She told me not to worry because she would have her pilot fly me back to North Carolina for the ceremony. Who could argue with this offer?

The next day I met with my VR supervisor and submitted my resignation. She told me that she had expected me to leave. She realized that it was hard to turn down a job in the private sector. What started off as an employee/employer relationship had evolved into a friendship. I really was going to miss her and the other friends that I had made.

Before starting my new job, I contacted Martha and Chandelier to see if they would be interested in going somewhere. Martha was still living in Florida and we decided to go on another singles cruise. No activity director there to lead you around like children. You just leave the port at St. Petersburg/Tampa, travel the twelve miles to international waters, set anchor, and for three days you drink, eat, dance and become acquainted with men whom you will never see again.

The room we shared was as small as a coat closet, but there was never a time that the three of us were in the room at the same time. This was about the third time we had been on this type of cruise, and we always enjoyed it. The three of us had traveled so many times together that we knew what the other was going to say before speaking. When we returned to shore, we went back to Martha's house for the night. The next morning, we left for our respective cities.

Chapter 9

Time to Start Planning for My Future

A few days after returning home, I left for Virginia to begin training. I stayed in a hotel about five miles from the office. When I reported for work the next day, I met the clerical staff, began training and reading the worker's comp laws and regulations of numerous states. I felt as though I was back in college. Oh wait, I really never studied in college. My work with the State VR was similar, yet it was entirely different. Margaret was a walking encyclopedia and never referred to any notes. I decided she must have had a photographic memory.

Even though I was apprehensive, I was glad to have a job in which I would be paid according to my abilities. Luckily, God had given me and I had inherited, many attributes that made this job perfectly suited for me.

After four days, I gathered my files and started my six-hour drive home. As usual, I put a 60s CD in the player and listened to my music. After being on the road about two hours, I was shocked into reality by the ringing sound of my phone. Who can ever forget the bag phones?

A friend was calling and reminding me that I was to stop by his house on my way home. Even though I was tired, I was not that tired. I had met Max when purchasing medical equipment for one of my clients, while still with VR. He was co-owner of a small medical supply company in Winston-Salem, NC. He was all of the things I was not. He was a mathematical whiz, totally settled, always though before acting, quiet, a non-drinker and without many life experiences. He was also noncommittal as far as relationships go and did not have much interest in any type of music. On the positive side, he loved Broke, was very sexy and willing to do anything to please me.

There were several reasons I chose to remain in North Carolina when offered my new job: my mother was getting older, Broke needed a baby sitter, I was getting older and I felt I needed to establish some roots.

After working about four months, I decided to purchase my first home. It was the typical starter home located in a small development about six miles from the city. City living, no matter how large or small, has never been of interest to me. Actually, I could live on an island as long as I had all the modern conveniences and accessibility to the real world when I felt the need.

There were many things about the house that I had to change before I moved in. The wallpaper was hideous, one of the bedrooms had hot pink carpet and the curtains were hideous. (I hate both carpet and curtains.)

I hired a contractor who painted the walls a neutral color, replaced the pink carpet with hardwood, enlarged the deck and had solid wood shutters placed on all the inside windows. It took about two months before I could move in.

All my furniture was a combination of antique and modern. Luckily, North Carolina is the furniture capitol of the world. After the market in High Point was completed, I drove to Hickory, NC and bought all new furniture. As I love the Oriental style of furniture, many piece were this style. The furniture was perfect for the new look in the house. One extra bedroom was used as my office and the other used for a den with a sleeper sofa.

My friend, Martha, owned art galleries and framing stores, located from Tampa to Naples. As I had helped her open her first gallery in Clearwater, she always sold artwork to me at her cost. I had acquired two works by Salvador Dali, one for fun and the other for investment. I also obtained several Oriental works of a geisha girl, a samurai warrior and several other prints by the same artist.

Martha is a good friend, and I admire her probably more than anyone I know. She came from the most humble origins, but through perseverance and determination, she finished college, married well, and on her own has been a millionaire numerous times over. I do not believe she even knows the words failure or can't.

The movers came and left, and several of my friends came over and we christened my new house. I love to entertain and have friends over, but I am so damn particular and compulsive about everything, I have often wondered why everyone keeps coming back.

Since I had the back yard fenced in, I was able to let Broke out whenever he wanted. My mother kept him from the time I left Monday morning to the time I arrived back home on Friday. As he was so little, I often took him on trips with me.

By Christmas, I was the top person in the company. The owner of the company, who seldom, if ever, spoke to his employees, called and asked me to meet him for dinner the following week. I had never seen him, but was told by Margaret what he looked like. I drove to the restaurant and walked in. Chip almost ran over to me, smiled and shook my hand. I was a little shocked because he was not what I had expected. He said that he wanted to meet the person who was making "our" company the most sought after in the southeast. He finished by asking, "What can I do for you?" As I always speak my mind, I mentioned that a raise and a new car seemed reasonable. Before I could say anything, he told me to pick out any car I wanted and that not only would I see a generous bonus, tax free, I would also see a generous salary increase. We had a few drinks and I left realizing that I was on the fast track.

I always felt that I would love traveling and staying in a different hotel each night, and now I had the opportunity. Of course, it was nice when someone else is picking up the tab. One month, Chip called me and told me he could not legally pay my bar bills unless I was performing marketing duties. From now on, I was to list any liquor as marketing. I had never charged for a meal while on the road so this seemed fair. From that day on, I became a member of the marketing staff also.

My paperwork was building up, and I needed someone to transcribe my notes and manage my satellite office in Winston-Salem. As luck would have it, Max had sold his portion of his company and offered to run my new office for a few days a week. All the other consultants in the field hand wrote their reports and mailed them in. I have the worst handwriting in the world; therefore, I dictated my reports and Max wrote them out.

After about six weeks, Max and I decided it would be more efficient for him to travel with me. This worked out perfectly, and in about a month he moved into my house. He loved Broke, and I was happy to have the company both on and off the road. As I am a controlling and demanding person, I did have some reservations. My thoughts have always been that the person who controls the finances controls the situation. Max never seemed intimidated by our working or personal relationship.

My territory included North Carolina, Virginia, Tennessee and parts of South Carolina and Georgia. As my reputation grew, I would travel to Arkansas, Alabama and some further areas in Tennessee, but only by plane. I was asked to work a California case, and this was the worst case I had ever had. The worker's comp program was bankrupting California, and after working this case, I realized why. I worked the one case and refused to ever work another one.

North Carolina, Virginia and Tennessee were mandated private rehab states, and their laws regarding the worker's comp programs were almost identical. All comp cases have the preponderance of going to court, and I seemed to catch most of the court cases and many ADA (American with Disabilities Act) cases. Now I was back on my own home turf.

I cannot think of anyone who has ever intimidated me, in or outside the courtroom. What I enjoy is the game of who backs down first. I know that part of my confidence comes from my experiences living through the sixties and the other I inherited. My cases rarely lasted more than a couple of hours, but while in court, I was losing money. My expert witness fee just didn't get it.

I needed to go back on the road and stay on the road. I decided to give several of my friends and co-workers from state government the opportunity to finally make a comfortable income. I hired "DD," Lynn, Devi, Randy, Peggy and several others.

Evidently, Margaret began to feel that I was trying to take her job. She knew that I had Chip's ear, and that he would allow me to do anything I wanted. I knew the only reason I had Chip's ear was the fact that I was helping him to build his company and helping him to buy larger yachts and jets.

Margaret continued to dislike me even more when Chip decided to give me a raise every three months and furnish a car for me. As the head of vocational services, Margaret not only received a percentage of the business I brought in, but she was furnished a new car every year and a jet every four years, if she wanted them. The strange thing was that Margaret could neither drive nor was she a pilot. Margaret was legally blind since birth, but I will give her this, she had lived in a sighted world for so long that she functioned as a sighted person. Very few people ever realized this about her. I did not really care what Margaret thought. I hate pettiness and do not have time for it. My main concern and interest was to continue to increase my income.

Within the next year, Chip decided that the consultants would now become employees and not independent contractors. He wanted to offer us a 401K and the benefit, so he thought, of taking out taxes from our paychecks. This ended up being a bummer for me. After I realized the amount of new taxes I was to be responsible for, I almost went into cardiac arrest.

I called my CPA and did learn some other tax advantages. I began to breathe again but I knew one thing, I would make plans to definitely retire early and retire outside of the United States.

The Christmas season was nearing, and the comp business was pretty much put on hold from the middle of November through the middle of January. I decided to begin my search for a suitable country to retire in. As I was on a mission, I wanted to travel by myself in order to concentrate on the business at hand. Max and I had discussed the tax situation and my dilemma, and he was in total agreement about leaving the United States and moving to another country.

I decided to travel through Europe and booked a flight the first part of December. As I had over three hundred thousand frequent flyer miles, the cost of the flights, the Euro Pass, and the majority of the hotels would be absorbed with the frequent flyer miles. This would be my first Christmas away from Broke and Max was excited about taking my place by playing Santa. This would also be the first Christmas not having my annual Christmas party. I saw some of my usual guests, and when I told them that I would be out of town, I thought some would actually cry. I heard statements like, "You can't go," "Where will I go now?" and "Your parties are the highlight of the season." I was flattered, but I was on another mission and nothing could change my mind. Max and Broke drove me to the airport and we said our good byes. I did not tell Max that I had arranged with Martha to meet her in the Canary Islands for New Years.

Chapter 10

The World Traveler: No, Just Me

I arrived at the Gatwick Airport and boarded a train to Victoria Station. By the time we arrived at Victoria Station the effects of jet lag were beginning to take over. When the train arrived, I slowly got off the train with my big suitcase and hailed a waiting taxi. As I was getting into the taxi I noticed a hotel across the street. I told the driver to take me there. He indicated he was not going to drive around the circle to the hotel, and said something to indicate that I should just walk across the grass. I said that I was not going to get out of his taxi and I would make it worth his while to drive around the circle. He mumbled something, which I am sure was not polite, but he drove me to the hotel. I am sure he thought as everyone else in the world thinks, "The ugly American has arrived."

I checked in and went directly to my room. I slept for about four hours and awoke in time for "low tea." After having my tea, I decided to venture out and go shopping at Harrods, then on to Piccadilly Circus and then to ride a red bus.

The reason I enjoy traveling alone is because I am not a typical tourist, and really don't like "touristy" things. I like to do and see what I want to see and then get on to business. To be honest, my friends really do not like to travel with me either. I always go off on my own, and I always get separated from everyone else.

When I go into a store I like to touch the fabrics. This is the way we do it in the states. I learned this is not the way shopkeepers in England like you to shop. This ugly American showed my ugly head again as I touched and picked up everything. The sales people were running around like "chickens with their heads cut off." I exited quickly and walked down the street to see what other havoc I could cause.

I rode the red bus and saw the sites I was interested in. I decided to stop at Seville Row and do some Christmas shopping. At Seville Row Company I bought Max a beautiful wool sports coat, (or as I was informed, a weekend jacket) and a pair of chinos, (I knew this name as it is the same in the states) which I had cuffed. I arranged for the package to be mailed and to arrive before Christmas.

I was getting tired and decided to do what I do best, stop at the nearest pub. I ordered a Bushmills, sat down at the bar and listened to the music. I stayed for about an hour, and decided to return to the hotel while I was still able to function.

When I returned to the hotel, I noticed that many more men had checked in. Of the years I had been traveling over the United States for business, I was accustomed to being the only female staying in hotels during the weekdays. Evidently this also was the same case in England.

When I found a seat, a man came over and asked if he could sit down. As I love an English accent, I invited him to join me. He told me that he was a sales rep and sold silver to businesses in England and France. I asked him if he represented the Sheffield Silver Company. He said that he did, and he would give me his card so I could take the train to Sheffield to purchase from the factory at his cost. Now, I was excited!

We had a couple of drinks, and he asked if I wanted to go up to his room and share a joint. I told him that I only smoked fags. As the British have a different humor than we do, he did not even laugh. I thought I was being funny.

He really did not have to make any small talk. I had decided before I left the states, that I was determined if at all possible, to sample a man from every country I visited. I had even brought my own condoms. Uncomplicated sex, with men you will never see again, is exciting and erotic. Thanks to the sexual revolution of the sixties, women now have the same freedom regarding sex as men, if they chose.

The next morning I visited the English consulate to find out all legal matters regarding foreigners relocating to their country. It was not very complicated, and it would be easy for Max, Broke and me to obtain any necessary papers. As this interview did not take as long as I thought, I had more than enough time to do some sightseeing.

I decided to hire a driver and have him drive me to as many sights as he could in the next four hours. If I decided I wanted to get out and walk around, I would call him after I had finished. After a quick and thorough tour, I decided that I would take the Thames River cruise and then return to the hotel. I had decided to visit the theatre district that night.

The next day, I had plans to travel to Paris by train. I wanted to travel by airboat but it was not available. The train car was elegant. There was one seat to a row and *Dom Pérignon* flowed freely. The meal was wonderful and the view fantastic. The travel time was so quick that I almost did not have time to finish by first bottle of bubblie. As I disembarked from the train, I wished I could have turned around and gotten back on the train. The station was filthy and beggars were everywhere.

I found a taxi and decided to take a tour as I did in London. This driver was not as cultured or helpful as the one in England. I did see the Eiffel Tower at night and the sight was beautiful.

I love any type of art, and I could have spent a month inside the Louvre. The Pyramid was the perfect contrast of modern architecture to old. Although I did not want to stay in Paris any longer, I will never forget these three sights.

When I returned to the station I checked the board with the train schedules. I decided I would travel to Lucerne, Switzerland and then to Geneva. After I traveled about three hours I spent the night, or what was left of it, in a small hotel across the street from the station. I woke up early to catch the train to Geneva.

I just knew that there would be snow on the ground. When I asked the taxi driver where was the snow, he told me, "You will have to travel to the Alps for the snow. We only get a few dustings during the winter months." When he asked where I wanted to go, I told him to suggest an older hotel on Lake Geneva. He suggested two and I chose The Four Seasons.

I checked in and decided I would make this my headquarters until I was to leave for Madrid. One of the perks of the hotel was a masseur who visited your room twice a day. After I visited the consulate and was told what I would need to live in Switzerland and what the fee was, I was set to see the rest of the country.

I took a train to Zurich via the Alps route and stopped by Gstaad to see the ski slopes. The next stop I was interested in was Zurich and to see the most guarded, safest banks in the world. I shopped and found that most stores, like the ones in Geneva, were locked, and if you knocked to enter, you better be prepared to buy. Of course, you were served any type of cocktail and many different types of pate or any sweets you desired. I stayed a couple of hours and bought a few things. I always buy some jewelry and clothes when I visit different places.

When I returned to my hotel, my masseur had left a message at the front desk requesting I contact him when I returned. I was ready for a massage and room service. I went to Switzerland thinking I could buy Rolex watches for cost at the factory. I toured the factory in Geneva, but to my surprise, the prices were not any different than when I priced them in the states. Oh well, the friends I promised a Rolex watch would just have to get one elsewhere. I did buy myself a Salvador Dali watch and some jewelry.

Most days, I would use my Euro Pass and travel to nearby countries. I did venture a little further when I visited Italy. I toured the Vatican and saw the now familiar Swiss Guard. I learned their story and watched them perform their ceremony.

The one country that I wanted to visit was next on my list. It is not actually a country, but The Principality of Monaco. Not only had I followed Princess Grace of Monaco, I had followed Formula 1 racing for over twenty years. I really wanted to rent a car and drive the course, but I did not have the time. I did want to go to Cannes and walk through The Carlton Hotel and imagine seeing Cary Grant walk into the lobby. Of course, Cary had died about eight years before my trip into the Carlton's lobby, but I still could close my eyes and see him.

As Monte Carlo is part of France, the laws regarding residency are similar, but Prince Rainier controls his principality. No matter where you go in the world there is one saying that always holds true, "Money talks and bullshit walks." Unfortunately, my time in this beautiful part of the world was over, and I had accomplished most of what I traveled to Europe for. I quickly traveled back to my hotel to pack, have a massage, call and see how Broke was doing, drink to my trip and catch the night train to Madrid.

I arrived early for the train, but did not have to wait long. As I had booked a sleeping car, I was ready to take a nap and wake up in the morning in Madrid. The sleeping car was not quite what I had expected. There were six beds in one room and one other person with me, for now. I knew that I was not going to sleep with six other people, so I found the conductor and immediately booked an entire car for myself. Of course, the cost was minimal. As it turned out, I was free of pigs, chickens and other farm animals as roommates.

The train finally arrived in Madrid about five in the morning. I hailed a taxi and headed for the airport. I arrived about thirty minutes before the flight left, boarded quickly and found my seat. The plane ride was about two and a half hours. When we were cruising at altitude, the seat belt sign was turned off, everybody started smoking and I ordered a stiff drink. The steward turned up the music and the Spaniards were dancing in the aisles. Flying on US airlines is entirely different from airlines headquartered in other countries.

I heard a dog bark, looked down and saw a darling Pomeranian who looked like Broke. I picked him up, and his owner came up to me and apologized. I told him about Broke and how much I missed him. He said that his Juan could sit with me for the remainder of the flight. I really enjoyed the remainder of the trip with my new "flying companion."

We landed in the Canary Islands on time. I reluctantly returned Juan to his owner, went to the baggage claim and then found a taxi. Although the Canary Islands are owned by Spain, they are located nearer to the coast of Africa. I decided that I would have to travel to Casablanca since I was this close.

Martha had arrived the day before, and promised that she would be at our villa by the time I arrived. I had purchased a timeshare about a year ago for the sole purpose of using the exchange program for my trips traveling out of the United States. I could not find one villa for a two week period; therefore, Martha and I would be using one villa for one week, and another for the next week. The complex we were staying at first was called Beverly Hills and our villa was located on Rodeo Drive. I knew that I would be in for a surprise.

When the taxi pulled up to Beverly Hills, I knew I was nowhere near the real Beverly Hills. I had asked for a first floor villa and found out that this Beverly Hills was more of a mountain than a hill. There were no porters, so I left my suitcase in the main building and started my climb up Mt. Everest. Martha was waiting at the top of the second flight of steps and yelled down to ask if I needed any help. Naturally, I gave her the finger and she started laughing.

By the time I reached the top floor, I felt as though I had, indeed, climbed Mt. Everest. I limped in the villa and fell on the sofa. Martha had a drink waiting for me and said, "You are going to love this. Look down at the pool." I got my drink and walked out to the balcony, looked down and realized that all the swimmers and bathers were nude. This was my first time where skinny-dipping was encouraged and legal. Martha was laughing because she knew that I loved going nude. I swam this way when I could and was not uncomfortable around nudity. Martha, on the other hand, was much more uptight than me.

After having a couple more cocktails, we decided to go to the main lobby and rent a car. There was only one car left and it was a piece of crap. As we did not have a choice, we rented the crap car and decided to explore the island. We were staying on the largest of the islands, Tenerife. The highway was well kept and the farther we climbed, the slower the car went. I really think I could have run faster than the car. When we reached the top of the mountain we found a place to park, went to the end of the road and looked down at the city of Tenerife. We were actually above the clouds. If we could have leaned over another two feet, we would have been able to touch the clouds. I could only look for a few minutes because I am afraid of heights. I am one of a small percentage of people who suffer from acrophobia, who want to jump as soon as they look down. I also have the added feeling of sexual arousal, which is much enjoyable than jumping would be,

As we were driving down the mountain, Martha never applied the brakes. For once the crap car was traveling faster than fifty miles an hour. We traveled all around the island and found the nude beaches. We parked and I pointed out to her that no one we saw looked like a model or movie star. Women seem to want to look in great shape before going nude. Men, on the other hand, really don't care. A man will go nude on the beach with his stomach hanging so far down that you can not tell if he has a penis or not. One thing for sure, he hasn't seen his penis for many years. The older I become the braver I am. For me, a nude beach is for getting an even tan, and certainly not for meeting a man with a big gut and a questionable penis. As Martha was the driver, I decided to come back to the beach later and go to the pool back at Beverly Hills for now.

Martha was ready to go out and try the different cuisines of the island. Martha loves the experience of trying different foods, eating in different restaurants and loves to experiment with good wines. I, on the other hand, am a drinker and do not really want to experiment with food or wine, but I am willing to go along for the ride. I told Martha to choose any type of restaurant she wanted, and I would sit with her and drink my dinner and probably have a dessert.

The next morning I went to the nude beach, got a great even tan, dressed and walked back to the villa. When I returned, Martha told me that she had found a new way to get to the villa without walking up Mt. Everest. I was all for it until I found out we would have to scale a six-foot wall. (Actually, we parked the crap car beside the wall and used it as a stepping-stone to climb over.) Who says ingenuity is only for the young?

Finally, the week on Rodeo Drive was over and we drove to another villa about ten miles further. I had never stayed at an inclusive resort and never will again. This type of arrangement is not for someone who does not care about food and doesn't drink rum.

Luckily, this villa only had about six steps before we reached the front door. This villa was much larger than the other one. The master bath had a large enough Jacuzzi for five people. The only disadvantage was that it did not work, and was never fixed before we left. As I have an obsession about dirty clothes, I used the tub as a washing machine.

We had a large kitchen and Martha, being a gourmet cook, decided to buy some groceries. While she was at the grocery store, I decided to go out by the pool, swim out to the bar and have a drink or two.

Martha came out by the pool to inform me that she was making a seafood dinner and flan for dessert. Both sounded good to me. I had never eaten flan but I love most desserts. The meal was delicious and the flan was wonderful. From that night on we ate flan all the time. I learned how to make it, but mine never tasted as delicious as hers.

We had found an interesting restaurant about a mile from the villa. Every day at lunch I had a salad and octopus. On one occasion, Martha, who speaks Spanish, was trying to communicate with the waiter and was asking him where the bano was. He did not seem to understand. She used every word that could mean bathroom and he still did not understand. I just happened to be looking around and noticed a door marked "toilet." I could not help myself, and I asked the waiter where the toilet was. He immediately pointed in the direction of the door marked toilet. Martha quickly turned around, saw the sign and called me a bitch. This is no insult to me and never will be.

I always go shopping when in another country, and I was chopping at the bit to do so now. We went to a building that resembled a type of mall. I wanted a lightweight jacket that I could use on formal occasions.

We shopped around and finally found a shop with leather goods and the type of jacket I was looking for. Martha told me that she would do the negotiating and I stepped back. A guy came up to us and asked where we were from. For some reason, we both knew if we said the United States, he would double the price. Martha started speaking with an Irish accent and I followed her lead.

I purchased the jacket for myself, and some pocket books for gifts. I know the prices were better than if we had spoken in our normal accents and mentioned we lived in the United States.

I told Martha that I needed some jewelry and we left for the main shopping district of Tenerife. Most of the stores were closed for siesta. We found out that they did not open until 5 PM. I did notice some stores that seemed to be open, and walked over to check things out. Naturally, I picked the most expensive jewelry store in all of Tenerife. The window was full of the most beautiful and unusual jewelry I had ever seen. I walked in, and was met by a salesman who was dressed very nicely and asked if he could be of assistance. He introduced himself as Amal. I told him that I wanted to look around, and he told me to take my time and asked if I wanted a cocktail and some pate (I thought I was back in Geneva.)

I told Amal that I would like a White Russian, and Martha spoke up and said that she would have one also. Amal sent an employee to get the drinks and the ice. Before the employee left, I told her that I might be here the rest of the day, and to get an extra bag of ice. I had learned traveling through Europe, the United States citizens may consider ice a necessity, but it is not so in other countries.

As I was looking at every piece of jewelry in the window and though the glass counters, I knew that I would indeed be here for the remainder of the day. The employee returned and was followed by a man with a silver tray with two White Russians. I stopped the employee, and instructed her that she really needed to get a bottle of vodka and a bottle of Kahlua. She looked at the owner and Amal noted that she should follow my instructions. She left and I looked at more jewelry, and told Amal to show me something very exquisite and a one-of-a kind piece. Amal motioned for me to have a seat and that he would call someone to bring this type of jewelry.

He left to make his call, and Martha and I settled down for another White Russian. Martha was not going to purchase anything. She was in one of her "lost a million" years.

Amal came back and started talking to us. I asked about his name, and he said in Egyptian the name meant hope. He was the seventh son of a seventh son. He told me that his six brothers also lived in the Canary Islands. We talked and he asked us about the United States, and why had we traveled to the Canary Islands. I explained that I had flown in from Madrid and Martha had flown from Florida to spend the holidays together.

A door opened and Martha and I looked around at the same time and noticed a very handsome man come in through the back door. Amal introduced the man as his oldest brother, Aadi. Aadi (which means first or one) had brought the type of jewelry I had requested.

One necklace just seemed to jump at me. It was indeed exquisite and a one-of-a-kind piece. I asked Martha what she though, and she commented that it was classic and looked like something I would wear.

We talked some more with the brothers, and they asked if we had seen any nightlife since we had been on the island. We said that we had been to a couple of clubs but were not impressed. They said that we had probably visited the clubs that the tourists knew about and not the clubs that the locals frequented.

We left with my necklace, the certified appraisal and dates for the night. We really had not been paired with either brother so we decided to flip a coin, and I won the older brother. Now we had to go to a nice clothing store and find something sexy to wear. We finished our shopping and returned back to the villa. We were both excited and felt like schoolgirls on their first date.

The clubs that Aadi and Amal showed us were all private and impossible to enter unless you knew the right people. Our dates were clearly the right people. We danced, drank and met the most interesting people. Night turned into day and day into night. Two days later, we returned to our villa.

Our vacation was coming to an end and I was really sad. I had called home and spoken with Max and Broke on numerous occasions, and was glad to be going home. As Martha and I were traveling in different direction, we said our goodbyes at the airport.

The first leg of my flight was full of people. When I landed in Madrid the connecting plane going to Atlanta was cancelled. I waited about seven hours at the airport before another flight was ready to leave. As I hate to wait on anything or anybody, I bitched the entire time to anyone who would listen. When we finally boarded, we were told something about having to fly over land all the way. I asked the stewardess how we could fly only over land all the way. Instead of answering my question, she offered me and everyone else on the flight free drinks.

The flight stopped in Iceland, Greenland and New York City, but no one ever disembarked. We changed pilots in New York City, took off again and I spent the night at a hotel in Atlanta. The next morning I few into Greensboro, but my luggage had other plans.

I arrived home at about midnight, three days after leaving the Canary Islands. Max and my mother asked me to stay at home for a while before leaving again. Broke just looked at me with those big brown eyes, and I decided that my travels outside of the country would be placed on hold for a while. My luggage arrived two days later.

I do not know whether I was tired or just mad, but I had to vent with someone. As I did consulting work for the airline, I called the personnel director to explain what had happened. He asked if two round trip tickets to travel anywhere in the world would pacify me. I told him that was a good start and he laughed. (I was serious.) We were to see each other the following month, and he agreed to have the passes ready for me then.

I called Martha the day after I arrived home, told her about my trip home and she said, as she always does, "If anything complicated happens, it happens to you. Maybe you should change your name to Murphy or Murphy's Law should be changed to Welch's Law." Her statement was actually true, but it did not make me feel any better.

On my first day back at work Chip called and asked me to meet him for brunch. He wanted to talk to me about handling some special accounts for him, and to see if I would be interested in volunteering for a couple of non-profits which he was stepping down from. I knew that he had moved to another state about eight months ago, and he wanted me to take his place in the organizations. I just looked at him, and asked how I was supposed to do the job I was paid for and take on two for free. I knew Chip, he did not do anything unless he benefited.

Our order came and he asked me about my trip to Europe, and said he felt sure that I would have contacted him in Germany. I knew he was in Germany for several weeks during the same time I was in Europe, but I really did not want to take the time to visit him. I changed the subject and asked how his trip was. He said that it was great but did not last long enough. He proceeded to tell me that he had crossed over on the QE2 and returned on the Concorde. I did not say anything, but I bet I enjoyed my trip more than he did his.

I discussed with him the fact that I was committed to meet with about fifty employers to help write job descriptions. OSHA was now demanding written job descriptions for every job, and I was asked by the CEO's and personnel directors of about twenty-five corporations to assist them. He said that he had forgotten about this, and was glad I had volunteer for the assignment. After I stopped laughing, I told him that he should know by now that I, like he, did not do anything without being paid.

He changed the subject and told me that some stock in the company was being released and did I want first option. I told him that I did, and that he could take the cost of the stock out of my percentage package. He agreed and we chit chatted some more and left our separate ways.

On our way out, he told me that he could not believe that I had gone to Europe alone with no hotel reservations and no definite plans of any kind. I told him that I never really thought about it one way or the other. He walked me out to my car and I noticed that he a bought a new Maserati. He smiled and said that I had bought it for him, and I smiled and said that he had bought my house for me. I knew that his car had cost more than my house but he did not know that.

I was glad to get back in my Taurus with my ten track CD player, and be able to listen to my beach music and play it as loud as I wanted. Actually, I was glad to be anywhere that I could play beach music. I loved my trip abroad, but I should have taken some CDs with me and I will the next trip.

For the next six months I was busy as I could ever be. Max and I were traveling our usual five days a week. Sometimes he had to complete my paperwork, and I would take a flight and leave him at home or at the hotel where we were staying. As I have always burned the candle at both ends, my physical health was being affected and I could barely walk on some days.

I had been putting off my hip and knee replacements long enough. I contacted Chip, somewhere in the Caribbean on his new yacht, and told him that I could not wait any longer. He seemed surprised that I would ever take off time from work. I told him that I would wait until our slow season and have both as close together as possible.

The last of October and the first of January of the following year, my surgeries were scheduled. I was going to have a second knee done in February, but my doctor refused. I looked pretty bad after the hip replacement and really needed to recuperate. Luckily I had great insurance and had twenty-four hour care during my recuperation period.

Max was kept busy on the phone and computer and doing reports for me. I had a business of my own, and he and I were trying to build it up so we could retire early.

One day Chip called and begged me to meet personally with a few of my customers. He was afraid that "we" might lose their business if they did not see me personally. He sent his plane for me and I met the pilot at the local airport. We traveled to see three clients in three different states, in order for them to see I was still breathing. Evidently, they were pacified and we left and flew back.

In June, my goddaughter graduated with honors from NC State. Max and I attended the ceremony with Ginger and Slick, their two other children and about twenty-five thousand others. We celebrated the reminder of the day and through the weekend in Raleigh.

When I officially returned to work, my caseload was busier than usual. Two things, money and more money motivate me. I immediately started to dive into my waiting caseload.

While I was out, Margaret had told me that she had completed the necessary papers for me to be grand fathered in several of the states I covered. Changes were being made regarding the requirements for vocational consultants, and I did not want to take the national test to practice in my field. As it turned out, Margaret had not turned in any paperwork for me, and I was given two years to complete the testing necessary to continue practicing. I have never done well on standardized tests and I was mad as hell with her. I have always hated a lying two-faced person. **A bitch** I can tolerate because then we are on even ground. The test was given only twice a year, and by the time I found out about the situation, one test date had already come and gone. To make a long story short, Margaret was asked to step down. **Payback is a mother!**

The next director was even worse than Margaret. At least Margaret had worked in the field and had been responsible for the private rehab field to even exist in most states. The entire organization was falling apart. Not only did we have a new director, we had a new owner and a new CEO, neither of whom I liked. I decided I would continue to work for the company until I passed the first test and the second test. I had forgotten that I had an iron clad "non-compete contract." As everyone has to be creative in life, I decided to take a six-month leave of absence, of course, with pay.

My good friends Francisca and David decided to travel with Max and me to Costa Rica to look for property and check out the country. Costa Rica is a hot spot for Americans to retire, and we had a good friend who lived in San Jose. Francisca and David were ready to find a second residence, and Max and I were ready to leave the United States for good.

I had used the exchange program with my timeshare, and we stayed in the largest villa I had stayed in to date. We traveled on the Caribbean/ Atlantic side of the country, and as the money exchange was more than we expected, we were ready to move. In Costa Rica there are meetings every week at different locations to explain to foreigners the advantages of retiring in Costa Rica. We were all sold on the move but Francisca was still working. She only had a few years left to get full retirement from state government, and did not want to forfeit her medical and retirement benefits. I could understand her reasoning.

Max and I really loved the country and decided that we would probably build a house and come for vacations until we moved permanently. We toured the Pacific side of the country also. This side was not as developed as the Caribbean/Atlantic side, did not have an airport but the beaches were more beautiful.

The four of us had the best time together. We climbed to the top of the volcano featured in the movie Jurassic Park, we visited an orchid farm and coffee/banana plantations. Unfortunately, our time was nearing an end, but we had taken full advantage of all the sights.

We checked with our friend who lived in San Jose, and he gave us some hints about relocating. Our friend, Tom, was most unusual man I had ever known. He could "step in shit and come out smelling like a rose," as we say in the south. Also, "Everything he touched turned to gold." He moved to Costa Rica in the seventies and made another fortune or three. He owned, among other businesses, a whore house/hotel in downtown San Jose. During the time we were there the hotel was sponsoring a contest to see which girl gave the best BJ. That was not so strange. The strange thing was that the grand prize was a trip to Disney World. I couldn't help but wonder, whether Mickey or Goofy would be the lucky prize when the winner arrived in Orlando. We left Costa Rica with all the information necessary for residency and the names of prospective contractors.

After being back home for about three months, Max and I decided to return to Costa Rica and marry there. Although Max and I were different in many ways, he was the most compatible, long-term sexual partner I had ever had. I was much more experienced than he, but he was a quick learner. When we were on the road working, we could barely make it thirty miles before we would have to stop at a hotel. We would then drive for about thirty more miles until we reached the hotel where we had reservations. This practice never got old nor did we ever lose our excitement for each other.

Unfortunately, Max did have some health problems that were pretty serious. He was told to stop smoking on numerous occasions, but just could not stop. Finally, he had a massive heart attack, which resulted in heart bypass. He stopped smoking for about a month or two, and then started back again. He never smoked in the house or the car, but the rest of the time he would sneak around. I tried everything I could think of to get him to quit. I think he felt that smoking was the only part of his life that he had complete control of.

Max had much to do with the success of my two companies and was my biggest asset. He was more sensible and realistic about life than I am. He had a calming effect on me, and I needed this type of person to help me keep focused.

I was still antsy about our move and wanted something to become finalized now, not tomorrow. We decided that I would travel again to Costa Rica and try to finalize our move. Of course, I am sure he just wanted me to leave to shut me up.

As I was able to contact my clients by phone while out of the country, he took on all the other responsibilities. If one of my clients needed one-on-one contact, he would be available to meet personally with them while I was gone. This was not his strongest forte, and I am sure he prayed that I could handle everything over the phone. I left in January of the following year with plans for our house and all necessary information needed to finalize the purchase of the house and land. I had contracted with someone who lived in a small town about forty miles from the Panama border. I landed in San Jose, rented a car and headed for Cahuita. The trip was about nine hours, and I stupidly left San Jose about 2 PM. I had no map, but some directions I had been given by Todd, the man who owned the land I was interested in. The entire trip consisted of driving up and down the mountains at night in a fog that never lifted. There were no hotels along the route, and the only town I saw was when I arrived at the bottom of the mountain.

I stopped once to ask for directions, and found out that the residents in the town of Limon were Orientals and did not speak much English or Spanish. I was in a catch-22 situation. I could not go back and didn't know where in the hell I was going, so I continued on.

I do not know how, but I found the bus stop with the red cement bench (the major landmark I had been given) about three hours drive away from Limon. I attempted to call Todd, but was unable to get reception on my phone. I finally found a small hotel, woke the owners and asked if they knew the Bakers. They shook their heads, so I rented a room from them.

The next morning as I was having breakfast, I noticed how beautiful the surrounding area was. There were lush plants, coconut trees and the greenest grass I had ever seen. In the middle of all this beauty there was a waterfall and a pool. My trip through hell had ended up in a heaven on earth.

I asked the other people having breakfast whom I knew were locals, if they knew the Bakers. The all looked stoned, and then I remembered where I was. There are no drug laws, and a person could snort coke and smoke a joint in public or anywhere else. The owner came by, handed me a phone and told me that the call was for me. I knew that I had several lost days and weekends in my life, but was completely sober now and no one I knew would be calling me. I took the phone and it was Todd welcoming me to Costa Rica. He told me that his wife should be walking in the gate right now. As it turned out, Todd's property and the hotel's property adjoined each other. The witch could have told me this before I checked in four hours earlier.

I had rented a house on Todd's property for the next three months. The house was large and surrounded by coconut trees. Todd had about two thousand hectares of property and a large portion was rain forest. He was willing to sell me four hectares for my house. The property also included two wells, and he would furnish the yard upkeep and the security. His compound was totally fenced in and had an armed guard who walked around the compound all night long.

Todd also owned a fern farm and sold to most countries except the United States. Evidently, the United States did not want the dirt of Costa Rica to enter their borders. Todd was developing a process of growing plants and tress without the use of dirt—not so much for the United States, but it would be cheaper to ship to his European customers.

A day in Costa Rica is divided equally: twelve hours of light and twelve hours of night. My first night on his compound was rainy, and I was sitting in the downstairs bedroom listening to an audio book. I heard something outside, and when I went to the window I saw a flashlight shining over the house. I decided to investigate his "operation" the next day.

I drove around the town and did find a dive shop. Since I had my accident I could not handle the scuba equipment any longer. I was limited to snorkeling, but loved any water sport so this was ok with me. While I was in the diver shop, Todd walked in and told me that he went diving every morning directly in front of my house, and that I could join him anytime. I told him to drop by in the morning and I would go with him.

There was also a money exchange, and I found out the U.S. money was going at an all time high. I exchanged $100 U.S. for 25K dolares. I went to the local grocery store, which is about the size of a large walk-in closet, and there was a little "grocery store" located every two hundred feet or so. Most are operated in the front of people's houses. I bought liquor, fresh fruit, vegetables and coffee.

Todd picked me up in the morning to go snorkeling and diving. The largest coral reef in Costa Rica is located in Cahuita and I explored it for the first time. Todd's boat was large enough to sleep six and had two powerful inboard/outboard motors. We were only eight miles from Panama by water, and Todd said he made a run at least twice a day. I told him that I wanted to go the next time, and he told me that as soon as we finished exploring the reef we would go.

In about an hour we sped to Panama to deliver his special merchandise. I had brought my CD player and CDs by The Four Tops, The Temps and other groups I loved. We had a great time and flew into the Panama dock area with my music blaring. The locals were so impressed with my music that I exchanged some of my beach and soul music for their reggae music.

I decided to tour a little. My great-great uncle helped build the Panama Canal, and was dry dock master of the U.S. side in the early twenties. He was also a contract deep-sea diver for the U.S. Navy. He was awarded a civilian Medal of Honor while in Panama for saving three men from a submarine that sunk in Colon in 1923. He was the most interesting man

I have ever known. After my tour, we returned to Costa Rica. Of course, the trip took less than twenty minutes.

My time seemed to be going by so slowly and I missed being around people I enjoyed being with. I called Chandelier and Martha and asked them to come for a visit. Neither hesitated and made plans to come the end of the week, but two days apart.

As there was no way I could make the round trip from Cahuita to San Jose in one day, Chandelier and I stayed in a hotel by the airport. When we returned to Cahuita the next morning, Chandelier could not believe that I found Cahuita in the daytime, and absolutely did not believe I found my way at night. To tell the truth, I didn't either.

I didn't tell Chandelier that when I left to pick her up at the airport, that I drove the same route as I had when I first came to Cahuita. I discovered that the dirt road I had driven on for about three hours was surrounded on both sides by water. When I arrived in Limon, I realized that the place I stopped to rest before continuing my trip was not an empty lot. I was parked at the edge of the dock where the cruise ships docked. I did remember that the car seemed to sway. I guess God was indeed, my co-pilot.

When we arrived at the house she could not believe the number of coconut trees. I told her that when a coconut fell on the ground that it eventually produced another tree. Of course, she noticed the Caribbean directly in front of my house.

As the house only had one bedroom on the first floor, she and Martha were to sleep on the second floor. This floor included two bedrooms, a bath, a kitchen and a large living room with an unscreened porch that gave the best view of the ocean.

After she put her things in her room, I gave her the grand tour of Cahuita. Cahuita is the only area in Costa Rica where there is a Negroid (their word, not mine) population that consists of fifth generation Jamaicans. The other residents are from about sixty different countries in the world, and the remainder consists of one hundred Costa Ricans thrown in for good measure. Cahuita's total population is about two hundred people and about one hundred dogs. The method of animal control in Costa Rica is too horrific for me to even mention.

Chandelier asked me why I, who loved all things perfect and had to have the best of everything, wanted to live in an area with no paved roads and was a day's drive from civilization. I explained to her that I wanted to be left alone for the remainder of my life, free of politics and the stress of continually working harder and harder just to pay Uncle Sam more taxes. She knew that Broke and Max were my biggest considerations and that I would never make any move that would jeopardize either of us. She did not even mention the living conditions, because she knew that I had no intention of living as the natives or the Europeans. She knew that I had always been a risk taker—some dangerous and stupid, but some very financially profitable. She also knew that I, like her, was stubborn as anyone could be, and that I was going to do whatever I wanted to do.

The next day we left for San Jose to pick up Martha at the airport. The flight was on time and we immediately left and drove to the hotel to relax before exploring San Jose. We left early in the morning to visit some local sites before leaving for Cahuita. On the trip to the house, Martha, like Chandelier, expressed the same opinions about the roads and could not understand how I could have made the trip by myself. I was getting a little tired of hearing about my inability to navigate.

Martha loved the piece of land I was going to purchase and the location to the ocean, but was unsure as to how I would ever become adjusted to living in this area. I showed Martha the rest of the "big city." As I had already made friends of all the lounge owners and was known by all the locals, everybody stopped to meet my new friends.

My favorite bar was at the end of the main drag and was situated partly in the ocean. The actual bar was carved out of a hugh tree in the shape of an alligator. The owner/bartender was playing the CD's I had given him, and told me that the people were singing the lyrics from the music I called beach music. I did hear the Tams and Four Tops in the background. He said he was teaching his friends the mojo of shag.

As Cahuita did have a resident witch doctor, I did not want him to think I was stepping on his flip-flops by introducing his flock to Satan music. I actually was a little afraid, if not a lot, of him. When he walked down the road talking to himself, everyone got out of his way. I am cautious of anyone who walks around in a long robe talking to himself, holding his string of bones and hissing at people.

I showed my friends a restaurant that was supposed to be delicious. They had never eaten in a restaurant with a dirt floor. When they ordered fish, a young boy behind the bar ran out of the restaurant. When he returned, he was carrying two fresh fish, a bag of lettuce, a bag of ice and two fresh limes. I didn't have to order. The ice and limes were for my vodka. Both girls said it was the best fish they had ever eaten, and by the time we left they had forgotten about the dirt floor.

Todd's foreman became our guide through the fern farm and anywhere else we wanted to go. He was also the person to call when we found an iguana in the shower, when the toilet overflowed, and when my friends found tiny pellets on their beds at night. The pellets ended up being bat turds that were used for fertilizer, but it took him about ten days to admit it to us. Just for information, coconut trees are a breeding ground for bats.

One night our guide took us out to dinner and I had king mackerel. I don't think I had ever had anything this tasty, as far as solid foods go, in years. While we were eating, I noticed something in the tree over our table. Our guide told me it was a sloth and that they caused much destruction. A asked him how in the world something that slow could cause any trouble. I watched the sloth the rest of the night move about an inch an hour. I think they are cute, but I think all animals are cute.

When we reached the house, I decided if I could sit and watch a sloth eat a leaf for three hours, it was time for me to go back home. I gave Todd my house plans, a certified check and made arrangements to travel back to the states on the same date as Martha and Chandelier.

My old enemy, weight, had returned and I knew that I would have to do something about it. Max offered to give me an early birthday present and send me to a fat camp. The official name was Hilton Head Island Health Institute. I don't care what it was called; it was still a fat camp.

As I had both South Carolina and Georgia clients, I decided to combine the two, work and pleasure. My good friend, Maddie, had graduated from law school years ago, and was the first and only female to practice law on the island. It would be good to see her, her family and her sister, Sharon.

The health institute was located on one of the many plantations on the island. I lived in a villa with one other female. As I arrived first, I took the first floor. My roommate was very odd, but I really did not socialize with her. I found plenty of people who were more to my liking. I walked six miles each day and ten on the weekends. I have not been in this great a shape since I was in law enforcement. We were all on the honor system, and could not have anything in our villas except water. All of our meals were prepared in the dining room, and we were given a total of 600 calories per day. We did not consume salt or alcohol. The people who smoked did not smoke for the seven-week period. As I was more active than I had ever been, I lost only twenty-five pounds, but I did lose a total of over fifty inches.

I would call Broke and Max every night to see how they were doing. I know Broke missed me, but I think Max was glad to have the peace and quiet. When I arrived home, neither Broke nor Max was there. I called my mother and found out that Broke was with her. She then proceeded to tell me that Max was in the hospital.

As I was about to leave for the hospital, Max walked in and said that he was sorry that he was not at the house when I returned home. He immediately led me to the bedroom where he had placed fresh roses and two champagne glasses. After we celebrated my homecoming and I drank a bottle of champagne, he mentioned to me that he was admitted to the hospital the day before with symptoms of a heart attack. I knew that nothing would keep Max from having sex, but even this was a little bizarre.

I did not ask if he walked out of the hospital before checking out because it was a moot issue. In a few minutes, he told me that his doctor said it was probably indigestion and they ran tests and an EKG. The test did not show anything strange.

We continued to celebrate until the doorbell rang. I got up and knew it had to be Mother. I opened the door and Broke came running in and jumping up and down. If I could have jumped up and down, I would have too. I asked my mother to come in, but she walked away. She hated Max (in fact, she hated everybody I ever dated) so I knew she would not come in.

The rest of the day and night I spent with Broke and Max. Max grilled a vegetarian meal for me, and steaks for himself. My life was back to normal and I was glad to be back home.

The next morning, I checked my messages and had a job offer from a company I was not familiar with. When I called the CEO, he asked if I would be interested in coming in for an interview as Director of Vocational Services. I arranged a time for an interview the next day. After discussing the Directors' position, I explained that I did not want the job offered, but I would consider a consulting position.

The director was a salaried position and I did not want to limit myself. In a consulting position, I could make as much as I wanted. We came to an agreement, but to sweeten the pot, I negotiated a percentage for bringing some additional work into the company by bringing in some former clients with me. I explained that due to some obligations, I could not start until the first of the next month.

Max, Broke and I needed to spend time together. Max and I had about three weeks of perfect bliss. During our free time we took Broke to the park and the beach. Broke really does not like to get sand all over him, nor does he enjoy the heat, but he loves to ride and he loves to play. Ever since he was a baby, he loved to play and would chase toys as long as someone would throw them to him.

Before I was to begin my new job, Ginger, Slick, Max and I took a trip to upper state New York. My beautiful and intelligent goddaughter, Amy, was graduating from college again. This time, she was receiving her masters from Syracuse University. Remember, her "smarts" came from me. We were all so proud of her accomplishments.

My first day at my new job was about to begin and I had bought a computer for Max to use. Before we were to start working, Max had another episode with his heart. He decided to see his specialist and was admitted to the hospital. The next morning he died under strange circumstances.

To make a long story short, I brought charges against the hospital and nurses on duty. Max's cardiologist encouraged me to bring a lawsuit against the hospital because he thought something was just not right regarding his death.

As neither Max nor I belonged to a church, the service was held at the funeral home's chapel. A close friend of Max's gave the eulogy and I was never so moved in my life. Max was cremated and had asked me to take his ashes to Costa Rica and drop them in the ocean in front of the house we were to build.

I have always been a take-charge person, and never really thought I needed anyone, but Max's death threw me for a loop. I do not know how I would have made it through the days following his death if it had not been for Ginger. She was a lifesaver, and I will never forget her friendship.

I decided to leave for a few weeks to help deal with my grief. A good friend of mine invited me to go on a diving/snorkeling trip to the Dominican Republic and I agreed to go. The trip was great but my heart was just not in it. I am sure my friend was glad to return home.

In two weeks I started back to work, but it was not the same. I cried on many of my long trips, and would return home instead of spending the night in a hotel. I had never felt the need for a man, but I realized how much Max had meant to me.

After a few weeks, Broke would travel with me and stay in the hotel while I conducted interviews with clients. Broke would be waiting for me to return with a treat for him. I would leave the television on in the room and music to keep him company. Of course, I would only leave him for a couple hours at a time before returning to take him for a walk. I stayed so often at the same hotels, that the manager or assistant manager would let him out if I were running late.

One day I received a call from the attorney I had consulted to handle the case against the hospital. I chose this attorney because he had won a settlement when he successfully sued the same hospital the year before. He had been reviewing the information I had sent to him and wanted to talk with me about his findings. He told me that I had a solid case, but it would be a long court battled and the costs I would incur would be enormous. He also explained to me since our marriage was not legal in the United States, I would not be entitled to any settlement, and all I would be doing is spending a fortune in order for his trifling family to benefit. I really wanted justice for Max and I wanted the people involved in his death to suffer, but I also had to be realistic.

Max always thought long and hard before he made any decision, and he would not have wanted his alienated family to benefit from his death. I decided to think calmly as he would have, and decided to drop the lawsuit. There was some satisfaction when the two nurses were prosecuted. Max was the third patient who had died while in their care (and I use the term loosely) under suspicious circumstances.

It was time to move on with my life. I had tried numerous times to call Todd and have him start on my house, but he never would give me a definite answer. About a week later, I received a certified check from Todd for the purchase price and an extra amount for my trouble. I never could reach him again.

I contacted another landowner in Cahuita and decided to purchase two hectares from him. We had the understanding that he was to find me a builder before I paid for the land. Months went by and the next time we talked, he told me that he could find no one to build my house. I asked if I could send a contractor/builder from the states for the job. He explained that would not work out due to the strict building laws of Costa Rica and the fact that all the laborers had to be brought in from Limon. I knew that no one in Limon spoke English and my plan just would not work.

I decided to put all my energy back into my work and to prepare for my future without living in Costa Rica and without Max. I knew that I was eventually going to move from the United States, if I lived that long. My fiftieth birthday was approaching, but I had not changed my lifestyle, nor would I ever. Full steam ahead is my only speed and risks are my way of life.

The day before the big day arrived, I took Broke and we went for a vacation of our own. He and I went shopping and I bought a new state-of-the-art stereo system, a new car, two pizzas and a bottle of Dom Pérignon. Broke and I then retired to our hotel where we shared the pizza and I drank the champagne. One can only imagine my surprise when I awoke in the morning. I remembered that past fifty would be the next day, so I stayed in the hotel the next night. When I awoke that morning I decided that my beneficiaries would just have to wait. Broke and I drove home with the top down and enjoyed our music.

During the last few years, my mother and I had established a better relationship, and I would take her on trips when I worked certain areas. I had traveled to Chattanooga, Tennessee on several occasions, and felt my mother would enjoy the trip. She asked a friend to go, and I booked a hotel near the downtown area in order for them to walk or take a cab while I was working.

I had taken the riverboat dinner cruise every time I had visited Chattanooga, so I invited them to go. I do not think either of them had ever been on a dinner cruise, and they loved this new adventure.

One of my clients told me that the new freshwater/saltwater aquarium had opened since my last trip. I decided we would stay an additional night in order to visit the new aquarium. We got up early, walked the short distance and stayed about four hours. To me, aquariums are just as captivating as museums, but with live creatures.

During the coming years I would take my mother and her friends many other places. They seemed to enjoy getting away and visiting other cities. One friend really enjoyed the trips because she never had to pay a penny for anything. As mother was Broke's babysitter, I had to hire a suitable person. I finally found someone and she worked for me for many years.

My house was getting a little small for me, and I decided to build a house on the lot my mother had given me. This lot contained our "dog cemetery" but I would never build my house near the cemetery area. I spent hours looking at plans and talking with architects. At this time, the interest rates were very low, but I just could not find what I really wanted and was tired of looking. As usual, I had to have what I wanted *now!*

I decided to remodel my house and add several rooms instead of worrying anymore about house plans. My house had the least square footage that any in my neighborhood. I found out the hard way that a remodel is more nerve wracking that building a house. I designed the master bath, my walk-in closet, the Florida room and a covered back porch. I added a section on the back porch for my hot tub and an area for outdoor cooking and entertaining.

As the bath is the most expensive room in a house, I was fortunate that Wills was a sales representative for a major plumbing supply business. He gave me his discount and I saved a fortune.

My Florida room contained a full service bar. I had a central stereo system placed in the house, as well as, speakers outside and around the pool area. The outside speakers were designed to carry sound only the distance of my lot. I never understood how this worked but it did. Instead of entertaining a hundred guests, I was able to accommodate over two hundred comfortably.

My annual Christmas party was still considered the event of the season, or so many people told me. The first Christmas after my house was completed I tried to book The Tams. Unfortunately, I was just too late with my request. Even without The Tams, everyone told me what a good time they had.

My life became taking care of Broke, my mother and working. The new job I had taken was great, and I was pleased with the management of the company and my contract with them. I was also doing contract work for the Social Security Administration, just to get my foot in the door.

Just when I though I could not possibly meet any more great people, I did. Because I always placed my clients quickly, I was given more and more cases to work. I no longer worked four states, but I was now handling cases all over the country.

One day I was having lunch with the CEO of a large corporation, and he asked me if I realized what an important asset I was to my field of work. I really was a little shocked and asked him to explain. He explained to me that he had watched me over the years, and was amazed that I possessed a natural ability to have dinner with leaders in the corporate world, conduct seminars with rooms full of upper management, and meet with blue-collar workers and treat everyone with the same respect. I was flattered that he had noticed this characteristic, but I knew in my profession, a person could only succeed if they treated everyone with respect. Of course, this is true in all aspect of life. As I was leaving he said, "Anne, you have moxie." I hoped this was a compliment, but I looked up the word as soon as I could find a dictionary.

Growing up in the south, we are taught to respect people and treat everyone with kindness. I am not saying that parents in other parts of the country do not teach their children the same values, but I can only speak from my upbringing.

After a couple more years of working my butt off and my orthopedic problems deteriorating, I decided to retire. I scheduled another knee replacement, and as a result of several serious falls, I was forced to schedule a cervical fusion. I was like the $8M woman but without the fine-tuned body.

While recuperating from the surgeries, I realized that I was going to have to consider finding another dog. Broke was fourteen and I realized, sadly, he could not live forever. Broke would never accept another dog in his house, so I made all the arrangements without his knowledge. I did not want another Pomeranian because I did not want Broke threatened by a dog that looked like him. I decided on another Spitz and searched the Internet for a breeder.

Finally, I saw exactly what I wanted and called the breeder. She sent me pictures of the prospective parents, and I placed my order for a female Miniature American Eskimo Spitz. As the parents had not been bred, I had to wait about five months.

My mother asked if she could name the new puppy. She said that she thought Powder Puff would be a perfect name. I agreed that name would fit the new puppy perfectly. When the breeder called to tell me that my grandchild (I had decided this puppy would be my first grandchild) was born, I was thrilled.

When I picked her up, she was the most beautiful dog I had ever seen, except for Efran. She was very calm and sat rigid on the seat and looked straight ahead. When I pulled into my drive she never changed positions. I thought maybe she was traumatized by her long trip and new surroundings. I lifted her out of the car and put her in the fenced yard. I then went into the house where Broke was waiting for me. I took him outside on the porch, and when he saw Powder Puff, he looked back at me with an expression that I am sure meant, "Get that **dog** out of my sight!" He then went back in the house and back to his room. I turned around and told Powder Puff not to worry. He will come around. Yeah, sure!

After a couple of hours Broke had still not come out to visit. My aunt came over to see the new addition and when she walked in the house, she came to a complete stop and said, "She is so regal." Actually, she did look at though she was a royal sitting on her throne. (my ottoman)

In about two days, Powder Puff's calm demeanor was replaced with excessive barking, stubbornness and demanding behavior. As she outweighed Broke by about three pounds, she took advantage of this situation. I was not a happy grandmother and thought about giving her away to Anne, a close friend of mine. Anne told me that she would take her, but advised me to give her another two weeks or so. Powder Puff did begin to calm down a little and quickly became the third member of the household.

I decided to do some subcontract work again. My mother kept Broke and I called Broke's former sitter to help with Powder Puff. Just like children, animals behave better when their parents are not around, and Powder Puff was no exception.

My new job did not involve as much travel as before, and I rarely stayed overnight. I only worked the cases I wanted and the locations I wanted to travel. After a while, I decided to retire again.

As I had become a certified mediator several years earlier, I volunteered at a mediation center in the neighboring county. I truly enjoyed the cases I was assigned, and helped out in this mediation center for several years.

Many of my friends lived within an hour's drive from me and we got together on a regular basis. Ginger came over about a weekend a month, as did Devi. "DD" had remarried, was still working in private rehab and would come over to relax when she could. My good friends, Francisca, Molly and Robin would come over for the day to swim and relax.

The children of my friends would also come over and bring their friends to party and listen to my music. My house became the party house for the mature crowd (present company excluded) and the younger crowd.

There has never been a dull moment in my life, and every aspect of my life was going well until Broke became very ill. On July 20th Broke passed away after giving me sixteen and a half wonderful years of love and devotion. Instead of burying him in the "pet cemetery," he was cremated.

It took about four years before I could pick up his ashes from Francisca's house.

Powder Puff and I became inseparable and I thank God that I have her and never gave her away. She is a handful and is the most independent and defiant animal I have ever seen. My mother told me that she was glad that I was finally getting a dose of what she lived with when I was growing up. **I guess now I was the one getting payback!**

Most families are dysfunctional and mine was no exception. I did have one cousin whom I was close to. Charles had retired also and we would do many things together. On most days at eleven o'clock, he would watch "The Price is Right." I, as everyone else, am familiar with this show, but I had not watched TV in years. Charles talked me into watching the show, and we would call each other to see if he or I could make the closer bids. He actually did better than me, but he also did most of the shopping in his house. One day we decided that he, his wife and I would fly to California to see the show personally.

After talking about our trip for weeks and watching the show, I started taping it every day so we could discuss it and our bids when we were on the actual stage. We decided to make definite plans. He was associated with several CBS affiliates and felt sure he could get us tickets and meet Bob. Before we could finalize our plans, he had a stroke and our plans were put on hold.

He recovered very slowly but he persevered. He started watching "our TV show" again and it helped him with his recovery. He did recover fully, and we continued to compare our bids and spent quality time together. We would also go shopping about every week.

I had always loved him and he was not only my relative, he was my friend. As we are so much alike in temperament and personality, it is a wonder we got along so well. We decided that it was time again to plan our Price is Right trip.

This time, I had to place our plans on hold. My mother had suffered another fall. My mother had been falling at least once a year for about four years. She would break a hip, her wrist or her other hip. Her will to live was so strong; she would always come back stronger than before.

This fall resulted in a broken neck. Even with this serious break, she came through the surgery as any thirty year old would. During her time in the hospital and at the rehab center, I decided to remodel her house and add some handicap features.

Her house was so cluttered and the furniture mismatched, that I threw away about everything in her house. Her family furniture remained. I had ramps built, her bathrooms made handicap accessible, had a gas insert put in her fireplace and changed her heat from baseboard to gas. She had always told me that she loved my house, so I bought furniture that was similar to mine. All the clutter was removed and I placed just enough furniture in each bedroom for her to be safe.

When she returned home, she was stunned and immediately fell in love with her "new" home. She never asked where her old belongings were. She sat down and cried and told me how much she appreciated everything. I was glad to do anything I could to make her life more comfortable.

She was able to enjoy her "new" house for about a year. She died from cancer about two months before her ninety-fourth birthday, and on her own terms, as usual. Her service was beautiful and as perfect as she wanted it to be. Of course, she had left precise instructions down to the verses to be read, the songs to be sung, the pallbearers and the door her family would use to enter the church. **She died and was buried under her own terms. She would have had it no other way.**

My sister came about a week before she died and we had time to discuss our strained relationship. As we had not spoken in about twenty-five years, we did pretty well in trying to begin to mend our relationship. I drove her back to Washington and we continued to keep in touch.

Not long after I returned from Washington, "DD" also died from cancer. She died surrounded by her children, John and Missy. "DD" had married the love of her life, Dal, and was finally happy in a relationship. "DD" and I were more alike than any friend I have ever had, and I think about her regularly.

In about six months, Charles also died. I was with him at the hospital, but did not stay in the room when his ventilator was disconnected. I just could not handle any more death.

After my mother's estate was settled, I decided it was time for Powder Puff and me to leave the United States. My house was put on the market and sold very quickly. I visited a friend of mine, Tiffany, who always said to me, "In five years?" This time I told her, "No, in one month." She almost fainted. My five-year plan had actually lasted almost ten.

Chapter 11

Powder Puff and Grand's Big Adventures

Powder and I left for Brasil from Miami, FL and I was able to get her a seat next to mine on the plane. As Powder was on her best behavior, all the stewards and the passengers seated near us fell in love with her. About 2:00am, one steward asked if she could take Powder to see the captain. I said that she could but prayed that Powder would not bite the steward as she picked up from her seat. Powder was gone about thirty minutes and when she was returned to me, the co-pilot was holding her.

As he put her in her seat, I asked if she had flown the plane because the ride seemed so smooth during the time she was gone. The co-pilot just smiled and gave me a pin with the planes' insignia. I asked if she were now a member of the crew and I was informed that from this day forward, she is to be known as "Pilot Powder".

I asked if we would be entitled to discount fares and he laughed and walked back to the cockpit. I wrapped Powder in her blanket and she and I slept through the remainder of the flight.

We landed in Sao Paulo, Brasil about 7:00am; the layover was only about three hours. Powder Puff and I stayed in the passenger lounge until an attendant came to escort us to the next plane for the remainder of the trip.

We had to travel five hours back in the same direction in which we just had flown. 9/11 guidelines state that any United States citizen entering Brasil must first land in Sao Paulo.

The plane, which was to take us to our new home in Natal, was not much larger than some private jets I had flown in. I had been unable to purchase Powder her own seat but she was able to sit in front of me on the floor. I know she was uncomfortable but I had done all I could to make her flight bearable.

When we finally landed, we were both happy to be on solid ground. I did notice several private jets in hangars before entering the main terminal. I decided, then and there, that I would meet one or more of the owners. I was able to go through the baggage area quickly because I had checked just one suitcase.

Alex, the translator hired by my realtor, during my first trip, was waiting for me. He rushed over to me and immediately asked where Powder Puff was. I just looked at him and thought, "No, kiss for me." (Brasilians always give you a peck on each side of your face)

Alex looked down, saw Powder and it was love at first sight. He picked her up, put her leash on and left with her to go outside.

I left to visit the foreign exchange booth. No one had told me that many US $100 bills do not pass inspection at the exchange booths. So I was stuck with about twenty I could not use.

We stopped by the grocery store and I stocked up on about everything in the store. I did not know when I would get another chance and I hated to depend on anyone. Alex drove me to the flat I had rented from my realtor until my house was built.

Maryanne, my realtor, who lived in London, had arranged everything to help make my move easier. Actually, she was to fly in the next week to help me become accustomed to the country. Until then, I was turned over to the capable hands of Alex and the attorney who was to assist me in all legal matters. I do not know what I would have done without either.

Junior, my attorney, escorted me to all the necessary offices to obtain all documents in order to finalize the purchase of my land, buy a car and buy a cell phone. In Brasil, your must have a CPF to purchase something as mundane as a cell phone.

The CPF is a small blue plastic card, which stores all of a person's information. I mean everything: from my parent's full name and occupation as they appeared on my birth certificate to the complete information as it appeared on my marriage license. Brasil is behind in some ways but beyond the States in many.

Brasil is known to have one of the best banking systems of any country in the world. It was explained to me that the CIA orchestrated the banking system in the fifties under the cover of the United Fruit Company.

Junior was so good to me and I assisted him in enacting some new and more progressive workers comp laws for Brasil. He became one of my dearest friends in Brasil.

Due to my poor planning, I had arrived in Brasil in the middle of their summer. It was hot as hell and more humid than I thought could ever be possible. To complicate matters, the flat I rented was not air conditioned, had no phone or computer service, no radio or usable TV and I had to walk up four flights of stairs to my apartment. This meant I would have to walk up and down the steps at least ten times a day to walk Powder. There were times I actually felt I would go into cardiac arrest and would need to stop and rest twice before I reached the floor my apartment was located. Sometimes I would wait on the landing on the second flight of steps for her to return. The steps were marble and sometimes she would slip, and sometimes I would actually sit on my butt and go down the stairs that way. The only real convenience was that I had a washing machine.

As my complex was surrounded by a wall and had a security guard, I began to let Powder out by herself and waited for her until she finished her business. This saved me from additional huffing and puffing.

I woke up every morning to the smell of food cooking (at least, I thought it was food) in the other apartments. The spices were so strong and sickening that I lost about forty pounds during the first month.

When my realtor arrived, she helped me find a contractor and had a phone installed. Unfortunately, her contractor did not speak English. I interviewed two more potential candidates and I hired the one who spoke English, Eddie. Eddie is a citizen of both Brasil and the United States.

I explained to him that I was going to build a house to accommodate my furniture and the house would have to be wired for indirect appliances. The house was also to be built the same style as if I were building in the United States. He immediately drew up the plans and I approved. The house would fit perfectly on my lot.

During my first trip to Brasil, I had purchased my land. The lot was narrow and deep. The back (where my bedroom was to be located) faced the Atlantic and the front faced sand dunes.

I chose a small beach community called Buzios, which looks like Myrtle Beach did in the late 50's and the 60's. The nearest city of any size to Buzios is Natal, which is about thirty miles, and the population is about two million people.

When Brasilians build a house, the workers stay from Monday morning to noon on Saturday. This means that the first construction is a small house for the workers to live in during this time. They bring a small stove, hammocks to sleep in and food to eat.

The majority of the houses in Brasil are made from cement block, wood is only used primarily in the roof section to hold up the tiles, few have ceilings, few are air conditioned and few have screens on the numerous windows. Most doors are made from trees found in the Amazon rain forest, are expensive to buy but are termite proof. Of course, the wood is supposed to be illegal to purchase.

My builder ended up being a liar and a thief and was fired. Junior and I decided that he would try to handle the situation and he hired a new foreman who also had the same redeeming qualities as the first.

When I was told that I had again been, "screwed and not kissed", I drove to my house, found the current thief and proceeded to fire him. Of course, I had to cuss him out in English and broken Portuguese. I have learned from traveling in about forty countries that when you use the classic four letter words and flip someone the finger, you do not need a translator. This gesture and these words mean the same in any language.

I also knew, by conducting business with lower class male Brasilians in the past couple of months, that they tend to be very passive and are afraid of women who sling their arms in front of their faces in an aggressive manner. He was no exception and did not stop backing away from me until he ran into a wall. He then proceeded to put his hands over his face.

This "ugly American" was about an inch away from grabbing him by his Brasilian balls and doing permanent damage. I knew I was not solving my problem but I enjoyed exerting my authority (which I had used little of while in Brasil) and watching the other workers see him slink away from me.

Now I was in the position of having to hire a new builder to complete the house. Carlos, my domestico (house person) knew some men from the interior (which is referred to as any location twenty miles from the ocean) who built houses and I decided to hire these people but under closer supervision.

Carlos arranged for the workers and he stayed at the job site during the week. Carlos had worked for me since I moved to Brasil and I felt he was lazy but honest. During my twice-weekly trips to Buzios, I never found him at the house but always at the beach. He was taking his "supervisor" job to the limit but I was in a "catch 22" situation, yet again.

In most foreign countries, especially Latin, Central and South America, you have to hire one live in, at a minimum. Carlos was my driver, housekeeper, cook, dog walker and many times, my translator.

My new workers were working quickly with the completion of my house and the time for me to give the ok for the delivery of my furniture was rapidly approaching. I had timed the completion of my house to coincide with the federal laws of Brasil regarding foreigners. A foreigner could not accept freight until after living in Brasil for at least three months.

I had been in contact via e-mail and telephone on a weekly basis with Global Direct Shipping, the company I had contracted with to ship my furniture from North Carolina. I had been paying the company storage for over four months. I was told, before I left the States, by Global that it would take thirty days after receiving the ok from me, for my furniture to arrive from New York to Brasil.

I immediately sent Global an e-mail but did not hear back from them. I called the three international offices in the United States, Toronto and London and their phones would ring, but I never got anyone to answer. I was beginning to panic.

About four days later, a friend of mine from the States called and told me that the FBI had raided Global, and legal action had been started. The other offices in Toronto and London were also raided by their prospective enforcement agencies but all offices were empty and looked as though they had been for months.

To say I was devastated is an understatement. I cried day and night for three days and then I became angry and decided to take action. I filed a claim with the underwriter, Lloyds, and contacted my local US Congressman and Senator.

I immediately heard from US Congressman Howard Coble and he assigned one of his aides to my case. Through his office, the FBI and the Federal Maritime Commission contacted me. The FBI was actually no help, but the Federal Maritime Commission was completely on the ball. This agency is the most professional, helpful and compassionate agency I have ever dealt with. I never heard from Senator Dole's office until a year later. I am positive this only occurred when she heard I was flying into Washington to meet with the Director of the Federal Maritime Commission. I really was surprised by her disinterest due to the fact that her job is to serve her constituents. Also, her mother and mine were members of the same church and had been friends for years.

Lloyds sent an investigator to access my claim, and he spent about six months before he turned in his final report. I spoke with him several times via phone and weekly e-mail. There was never a question as to the legality of my claim, but for reasons that were available long before the six-month investigation, my claim was denied. The Lloyds investigator hinted that I should file a claim with my homeowner's insurance. Of course, the amount of my coverage with Lloyds was three times that of my homeowners.

I felt that I needed to meet personally with the adjustor for my homeowners and made a trip back to the States. This company paid out the claim within three months of my meeting with the adjustor. It is impossible to handle business matters while living in another country such as Brasil. I had chosen Devi as my POA when I left the states. When my loss occurred, she dealt with the insurance companies and their attorneys. Devi had been a close friend for over twenty years. She, like I, had owned and managed several businesses and she appeared to have a good business head. Unfortunately, I discovered later that she had an ulterior motive for agreeing to be my POA.

My home is Brasil, which I built and designed to accommodate my furniture would never be home to me. When my mother died, I inherited priceless pieces from her family that dated back to 1800. When you lose everything, nothing ever seems the same again. For years after my loss, and even to this day, I think I will see something of mine somewhere and be able to trace it to the thieves.

There were many perks to living in Brasil. My days were spent snorkeling, swimming with the dolphins, drinking at my local bar and lying on the beach. Every Wednesday I would travel to the Natal docks and buy fresh shrimp, crab, lobster and fish. The names of the fish I never could pronounce. About three nights a week, I would travel to Natal to eat sushi and meet friends at the Natal Yacht Club.

Every weekend was one party after the other. Sunday was my day to entertain about 100 guests. I chose Sunday because my best Brasilian friends, my doctor, my dentist, my loyal taxi driver and Powder's vet were off on Sunday. My parties always included a very diverse group from the local elected official to my favorite bartender. My main requirement was that a large number of my guests had to speak English.

On Fridays and Saturdays, two other friends would entertain at their homes. This continued every weekend during the summer months. (the middle of September to the middle of March) Brasilians love to party, drink, eat and dance to their salsa music.

As I listened to their salsa music and attempted to learn to dance to it, I introduced my guests to the shag, 60's beach music and to "Willie, Waylon and the boys". I taught many to shag to the great song by Jerry Butler, "He will break your heart".

Roman, my taxi driver would play the CDs that I had burned for him and his reputation for good music enhanced his business tremendously. He introduced every Brasilian and most visiting Europeans to the Four Tops, Willie Nelson and the original beach music by the Tams and many other great groups.

One night I went out clubbing with several of my Brasilian lady friends. I was told that this club was for people between the ages of forty-five and seventy-five. At 4:00am, I fell asleep at the table. I was awakened at 5:00am in order to go home. I asked my friends, "If the older people left at sun rise, what time do the younger people go home"? I was told that the younger people would stay for days. As I said, Brasilians love their music and to party. On a personal note, I decided I would be more suited at a geriatric club, if I could find one.

One thing I remember about that night is that I was introduced to the national drink of Brasil, Caipirinha. It is a combination of one third sugar, one-third fresh line juice and one-third Caipirinah. After the second drink I experienced shortness of breath and never tasted Caipirinah again. I decided that my standard vodka, lemon and ice was enough for me.

I began running into difficulty regarding my permanent residency status. Before I moved to Brasil, I had traveled to Miami to meet with the Brasilian consulate in order to obtain all necessary legal documents for me to become a permanent resident. Every paper was stamped, translated and approved by the consulate before I left the states.

When I arrived in Natal, I registered with the police federal and was told, in no uncertain terms, that the Brasilian consulate in the United States does not control Brasil. The police federal control Brasil and I had to abide by their requirements, which were entirely different from the requirements of the consulate in the states.

I was given the name of the best Brasilian immigration attorney to check out the new papers I needed and to do all the legwork necessary for my permanent resident status. He spent months working on my case and I spent a fortune. Of course, I had already spent a fortune since I arrived in Brasil trying to obtain my permanent residency. This amount also included my home, which I was told would count toward the amount of money I had to invest in Brasil to become a resident.

Marrying a Brasilian ended up being the only avenue left to meet my goal. Europeans marry Brasilians all the time to obtain their residency and the practice is very lucrative for both parties.

All of my friends attempted to find a suitable man for me to marry. In Brasil, when you marry legally, both parties are required to sign a prenup when you apply for your marriage license. There are two types of marriages in Brasil, legal and illegal. Most Brasilians marry illegally (in a church) but all foreigners must marry legally (by a judge). Once married legally, the foreigner must remain married for one year before obtaining a permanent residency.

As I was facing deportation, I decided to see if Carlos were interested in getting "married". He jumped at the chance, and after talking to him to be sure that he clearly understood what I meant, we closed the deal. I made one more short but necessary trip, to the states. When I returned, Carols and I were married in his hometown. I brought my CD player and we were married with Willie Nelson singing, "Unchained Melody", in the background.

We had over seventy-five people at our reception. One man asked when we were going to start a family. Before my translator could say anything, I informed the man that I had a child and didn't want anymore. Evidently this guy must have thought I was still of childbearing age and that Carlos and I were hot and heavy for each other. I had just turned sixty and Carlos had just turned twenty-seven.

I would have thought, "I had died and gone to heaven" if I had been sexually attracted to him. I had never thought of him in any sexual terms. As a matter of fact, I thought of him as asexual.

After two months of being married, I traveled back to the states to help with my two friends, Liz and Maddy. Both had been diagnosed with cancer and I wanted to help in any way I could. I planned to stay one month with each friend and then return to Brasil.

Liz did not make it but gave it one hell of a fight. The unusual thing about Liz is that she had been one of the most negative people I had ever known. After she was diagnosed, she became the most positive person. I guess knowing that you are going to die, does that to you. Maddy is still fighting the beast even after three different bouts with cancer.

While in the states, I discovered that my POA, Devi had ordered a supplemental American Express card using my account and had charged over $10K. When I found out, she told me that she had not done this. When I approached Amex, I learned that Devi, using my identity, had written a letter to Amex to secure the additional card.

When I approached Devi a second time, all she could say was that she needed the money. I guess all the times she told me I was too trusting and honest for my own good, she knew me better than I knew her. If she had asked, I would have given her the money.

She arranged a payment schedule, in lieu of a lawsuit, although she never repaid what she took. My attorney revoked her POA and I chose my friend, Chuck, to handle my affairs. One thing about Chuck, he is honest and truthful beyond a doubt. He still acts as my POA.

When I returned to Brasil, Powder Puff, who had been suffering a skin disorder since we arrived in Brasil, actually had hair again. Carlos seemed happy and content and we started planning for my annual Christmas party and the expected arrival of my sister, Sandy and her friend during the month of March.

As I had some extra time and my doctor and vet had begged me to redecorate their houses, I decided to do something I had always enjoyed and had a knack for. Both wanted my "American look". I decided to take the job in exchange for free medical and veterinarian care for the remainder of my and Powder's life.

I added an addition to my vet's arrangement. This included not only Powder but also any additional dog that I would have. He also agreed to take care of Powder when I died. I knew he loved Powder and would treat her as his own.

My vet and I talked at length about the horrible treatment of animals in Brasil and the fact that spaying and neutering was almost unheard of to most of the Brasilians. His office always performed both procedures for free for any stray animal or an animal brought in by someone who could not afford the procedures. I told him about the DJ&T Foundation started by Bob Barker and told him that I would check their web site and help him complete the paperwork. When I checked the site, I learned that the foundation only assists vets in the United States and Canada. Oh well, I tried.

After Sandy and her friend arrived at my house, they planned to travel to Rio and I arranged for Carlos to escort them. Rio is a popular but dangerous city. All of my European friends no longer stay in Rio but in Natal. Natal has two carnivals a year and each is very popular and heavily attended. Sandy and Ruth had a nice trip but when they returned, Carlos was not with them. He had decided to have a good time in Rio with my credit card, which I did not find out about until the following month.

My sister and I decided to travel to Bier and take in the sights. After staying a few days, I decided I should have settled in Bier rather than Natal. Oh well, too late now.

When I returned, I learned that about R$30,000,000 was missing from my safe. I immediately accused Carlos and he said that he did not take it and went into elaborate details about the "local Buzios thief" coming over to my house while I was gone.

I went to the "Buzios thief's" house and he was putting on a new roof and adding rooms to his house. This man did not "have a pot to piss in or a window to throw it out of" but I still did not believe Carlos for one minute.

I was too tired in dealing with anything anymore. I was waiting for August when I became a permanent resident and for September when I could begin divorce proceedings.

After Sandy left, my year of marriage was approaching. I felt, after several years of worrying and constant struggle with the government of Brasil, Powder Puff and I could now settle legally in my chosen country.

Evidently Carlos had other ideas. Two months before my residency was finalized, Carlos decided to blackmail me or go to the police federal and tell them that we were separated. This would automatically revoke my application for residency. What surprised me is the fact that Carlos was not the brightest coconut on the tree but he had devised a plan to extort money from me and had thought it through.

After Carlos professed his love for me and Powder, he told me that his uncle had told him to get everything he could from me and then confessed to me that he had stolen my car and the money from my safe. As I was kicking him out of my house, I asked him if his uncle were going to spend the twenty-five years in prison for the grand larceny charge for forging my signature to the title of my car.

The next morning, I drove to Natal to file a police report. Carlos was arrested and spent the next several days in jail. The Brazilian jails are about the worst in the world. I may have been deceived but I knew for sure that Carlos was butt-fucked for three of the longest days of his life.

The police federal allowed me six months to get my affairs in order before leaving Brasil. I was given back my car but the money was long gone.

After Carlos left, I hired another domestico who had a wife and a small son. My domestico did not speak English so I enrolled him in classes. He attended for six weeks and spoke less English than I did Portuguese. I kept my sanity knowing that I would only have to put up with him for several more months.

Before the mess with Carlos had begun, I had scheduled a complete face-lift and some additional cosmetic surgery. My doctor told me that given my time restraints, I would only have time for one procedure. I chose the face-lift.

Brasil is known for their cosmetic surgeons and I had been referred to the plastic surgeon of the stars. He had his main office in Rio but he maintained a satellite office in Natal. His wife, also a noted plastic surgeon, worked with him.

After the surgery was completed, his wife invited me to come to Rio for the other surgery. Before I could answer, she said that I could bring Powder Puff and stay with them at their home in Buzios to recuperate. Not my Buzios, their Buzios. Their Buzios was located outside of Rio that Brigitte Bardot made famous and where the homes average $100m. Now Onassis' granddaughter has made this Buzios famous again by building her home there and raising the home prices another $50m. I thought this was a wonderful gesture but I explained to my friends I did not have the time at present. They insisted that I come back and I told them that I would someday. This is the manner in which many Brasilians treat their friends.

About a month before leaving Brasil, I met the nicest lady while waiting in the line at the post office. Marylu heard me speaking to the postmaster and when I completed my business, she came up to me and said, "Your accent sounds as if you may be from Charlotte, NC." I looked at her as though she had just landed from Mars. She noticed my odd expression and told me that she had lived in Charlotte for ten years and had just returned to Brasil. For the remainder of my time in Brasil, Marylu and I became very close friends. I offered to let her move in my house when I left; she seemed very grateful and is still living in my house.

I was ready to get rid of my family of squatters. They had lived off of my generosity for long enough. I have always paid my workers (in Brasil or anywhere else) more than the going rate. I have always been, like my father, generous beyond a fault. Sometimes this practice works and sometimes not.

My friend Mark agreed to handle my financial matters when I left Brasil. As we are involved in other business matters, he is the ideal person for this job.

When I left the United States, I knew that I could never bring Powder Puff back into the states from Brasil. For some reason, the states have very harsh regulations regarding bringing animals in from other countries. I only wish the United States government had stricter immigration laws for allowing anybody and everybody to move to the states to receive more benefits than the actual citizens. Oh, I forgot, no politics.

My good friend, Lex, who lives in Amsterdam, invited us to come stay with him until I could decide what I wanted to do. Lex and I always got together when he made his monthly trips to Natal. When his daughter traveled with him, they would stay at my home. Lex is one of the many people who have entered my life, whom I will never forget.

The first time I met Lex he was with his daughter and her two bodyguards. It wasn't the bodyguards I noticed, but the odor that followed them as they entered the restaurant. Many Europeans do not take baths as frequently as we do in the states.

Amsterdam is a beautiful city, and I know that I could be happy there and easily adapt to living there. Visitors from the Netherlands are the majority of tourists who visit Brasil regularly, and I had met many of them through my time in Brasil.

My friends in England and France made the same offer as Lex, but I felt I needed to move closer to the United States until I could decide "what I was going to do when I grew up." Powder Puff and I were not getting any younger. When Sis, a close family friend in Toronto insisted that we move there for a while, I jumped on the offer. I shipped some personal effects to Toronto, and I made plans to begin our next adventure. We were moving from sand and palm trees to snow and polar bears.

Mark made arrangements for us to stay a few days in Sao Paulo to rest and enjoy the city. The hotel he chose was very near the airport and the city proper. Powder Puff was the only four footed friend who had ever stayed at this five star hotel. Many times the concierge would walk Powder and dog sit while I explored one of the largest cities in the world. Brasilian statistics show that Sao Paulo is the home for over twenty million people, but not the international stats. I'll go with the Brasilians.

On the flight to Toronto, Powder Puff had to ride "baggage class." Air Canada did not allow me to purchase a seat for her, nor did they allow animals to fly in the passenger compartment. I should have called Lex and told him to fly us to Canada. We landed in Pearson International Airport early the next morning and I could not wait to go through customs and then to the baggage department to find Powder. I had to have documentation regarding her rabies shots and a general health certificate completed and translated into English prior to leaving Brasil. As Canada had no quarantine restrictions, I was more than happy to do anything necessary.

Sis was waiting for us in the terminal. I was never asked by any customs or immigration personnel to show any paperwork regarding Powder. I had more difficulty getting through immigration than she did. Go figure?

Driving from the airport, the first thing I noticed was how immaculate the highway and the entire city looked. Unlike the states, Canadians are very conscientious regarding several issues. One is the environment and the other is to maintain the true beauty of their country. Actually, they are diligent of many more important issues.

I settled in with my friend and she showed me around Toronto. Sis is a very active person and is involved in many things. She attended water therapy three days a week and I attended classes with her. During these classes, I met the best group of ladies I have ever known in my life and the nicest two men, Bill and Ted. Canadians are like no other people on earth: they have the biggest hearts and the warmest personalities, 'eh?

After our classes, we would always meet for coffee and conversation at Tim Horton's. (Krispy Kreme of Canada) I was usually the first to arrive and would put several tables together to accommodate "the ladies." Most of the time, we would sit and drink coffee for hours. Many of the ladies, Norma K. and Betty C. would make fresh cookies and other sweets at least once a week.

About once a week, Wanda, Ruth, Betty, Mary, Beryl, Betty and several other girls and I would go out for a meal and a movie. Most of the girls were older than I, many divorced or were widows, and some were lucky enough to still have their husbands.

I decided to stay in Canada and rented a high rise for a year. The view was great and faced the skyline of downtown Toronto. This view was the motivation I needed to begin writing my book. I knew what I wanted to write about and felt the title would come to me sooner or later. I spent much of my free time trying to put my words in some perspective.

Powder Puff was known as the "devil dog" of the complex. Her reputation traveled long and far. I hired a dog walker and Ms. Judy (Powder really loved her) would even have a hard time with her. I remember what my mother always said to me about Powder being just like me and she truly is. Her stubbornness, nasty attitude and loud mouth, are only surpassed by mine. Of course, her sweetness, kindness and loyalty are also inherited from me: she and I aren't all bad.

As I fell in love with Canada and its people, I completed all the necessary paperwork to become a resident. My application was denied and I had to leave for a short time to satisfy the border guards. I had to travel to the United States for several weeks before returning to Canada. Powder stayed with Sis and both seemed to enjoy each other's company. Sis was a good friend to do this favor for me.

While in the states, I decide to buy a car. As I was driving by my bank, I decided, for some reason, to stop and check on my credit score. I learned of other problems that occurred during Devi's tenure as my POA.

To my surprise and astonishment, Devi had stolen my identity and ordered credit cards and charged them to the limits. She also never paid the few bills (electricity, gas, phone and TV) which were due the month following my departure from the states.

When I opened my safety deposit box (which I had not opened in several years) I discovered I was missing my gold coin collection and several other valuable coins. The main theft was approximately $375K in cash she stole.

Devi always professed to be such a Christian, but in reality she is totally amoral. Needless to say, she had ruined my credit for life. I hope she rots in hell and I am there, just for a short time, to throw in the coals. Hopefully the sins of the parents are indeed passed on to her children and to their children.

I contacted two attorneys and each told me that the fee for handling my case would be over $150K. This would be, "throwing good money after bad," and I was not going to waste any more money on Devi. I contacted the district attorney in my county of residence in the states, but he informed me that, in cases such as mine, the state would end up losing money with the time they would spend prosecuting the case. Devi had covered her bases and was judgment proof. The name "sucker" which appeared across my forehead in Brasil was appearing again. I wanted my more familiar name, "bitch" back. I had worn that name proudly for many years.

My life was in Canada now, and I decided to make the most of it. As I would be driving my car this trip, I asked Molly to ride with me. The night before we were to leave, I stayed with her and Stumpie. Being in their basement is like experiencing the 60s all over again. Everything from our wonderful decade is displayed there. Stumpie is also the perfect example of a preppy, and I have never seen him without Weejuns, (no socks, of course) khakis and starched shirts.

Molly was the navigator and we made the trip in less than thirteen hours. She had never been out of the United States and I was glad she was able to experience Canada first.

We were lucky to get tickets for "Jersey Boys." Musicals have never been a favorite of mine, but Frankie Vali and the Four Season are of my era, and the performance was fantastic. We also toured the city of Toronto in a bus/boat. We actually traveled off road into Lake Ontario and then back onto dry land. Our trip to Niagara Falls was fun and we took advantage of every sight. We both lost sight of each other while investigating under the "falls." She knew that I always became separated and we had an alternate plan to meet at the entrance when we were finished the tour. We had opportunity to act silly, as we had when we walked on the beach at Ocean Drive, the summer before we began high school. She just had to leave too soon.

Toronto is the first international city I have ever lived in. I like their theater district much more than that of New York City. I attended many plays, another musical, "Dirty Dancing" and numerous other functions. The museums in Toronto are fantastic but my special interest was anything to do with the aboriginals. Aboriginals are very active in the Canadian culture. I am not saying that there is no discrimination against their "first people," but the Native Americans in the United States are not treated as well as they are in Canada.

I bought many original works from the aboriginals, and spoke with many of the artists about my ancestry and the small amount of Native American blood that flowed through my veins. Several commented that it was obvious that I did have signs of being part aboriginal, and I began to feel a special kinship as I spoke with them and saw their many colorful tapestries and original artwork.

Toronto is very "artsy" and has its own international film festival. I had decided to attend this function and the sci-fi convention. At the sci-fi convention, I met the actors of Stargate SG1, my all time favorite, Leonard Nimoy, and a multitude of others. As a large number of television shows and movies are filmed in Canada, it is not unusual to see well-known actors almost daily. Many studios in the states have found Vancouver, BC the perfect location to make films. Vancouver is an area where you are able to find miles of snow-covered mountains and snowdrifts, and beautiful clear lakes and streams within a short distance of each other.

Although I have never understood Shakespeare, I attended the festival in Stratford, Canada. This festival continues for months, but I wanted to attend the performance of Caesar and Cleopatra. Christopher Plummer was playing the role of Caesar and I wanted to see him perform in legitimate theatre. I am probably one of the few people who has never seen "The Sound of Music." As I was watching some movies on television while living in Brasil, I discovered Christopher Plummer and his great talent. I found out that he was Canadian and would be appearing in the Shakespeare festival within the next couple of months. During this time, he was also having his book signing in Toronto.

I met him after the play and he is a very humble man. I spoke with him again at his book signing. Aside from Cary Grant, he is the most classy and sophisticated actor that has ever walked across a stage. It also seems, like Grant, that he was never truly appreciated by Hollywood.

Within two months, my friend Robin flew to Toronto, but we did not have the fun Molly and I did. She came to drive me back to North Carolina in order for me to have emergency surgery. I had fallen at my complex while walking Powder, and cut a large portion of my calf off.

My good friend and plastic surgeon, David, was waiting for me when we arrived in Concord, and operated the following morning. I stayed one night in the hospital and recuperated at the home of Robin and Chuck. Their daughter, Ellen, helped me with the bandages and my medical care. All four of Robin and Chuck's children are very special to me, but Ellen is one of the kindest and sweetest young girls I have ever had the pleasure of knowing.

When seeing my orthopedic while in the states, I was completing the usual mundane forms. When the question was asked, "Have you ever taken illegal drugs,' the best answer I could think of popped in my mind. What can I say? I'm a product of the 60's. The dilemma of my searching for the title of my book was now solved.

When it came time for me to return to Canada, Chandelier drove me back. Unfortunately, she had to visit all the sights by herself, but we still had a wonderful time together. Chandelier is as independent as I am, and is able to do everything on her own. Sis, the official tour guide, drove Chandelier all over Toronto, as she had Robin and Molly.

Sandy, my sister, came for Christmas and I decided to have a Christmas party. About fifteen of my pool buddies came and so did Bill and Ted. Everyone said they had a great time, and we drank, listened to 60s Christmas music and enjoyed being with each other.

As I knew I was going to have to leave Canada soon, I started to make plans to move back to the states. Since Devi had ruined my credit, I was fortunate enough to have a friend who had rental property. Allen was willing to rent to me without a credit check. We agreed that I would move in his rental house the later part of November. Several of my Canadian friends wanted to have parties for me before I left. Bill and his wife Pat had a cookout. Lorraine and Ted had a coffee party and invited about thirty of the "pool buddies." Both of the parties were great and the weather was cooperative.

I had to make arrangements for my furniture (Yes, I had to buy all new furniture for my apartment in Canada.) to be shipped to the states. I was a little hesitant; I did not want anything stolen again. I contracted with a company that I checked out with several law enforcement agencies and decided that they were reliable.

As soon as I reached my "new, old hometown," I took Powder by her U.S. vet. I had called Dr. Tim several weeks before leaving Canada and told him that the vet in Canada thought that Powder might have Cushing's disease. Dr. Tim drew her blood, and sent the sample to the University of Tennessee, the only facility in North America which tests for this disease in dogs.

After Powder's blood was drawn, we drove to visit Maddy in Hilton Head and Chandelier in Savannah. I had about a month to wait until the delivery date of my furniture. While we were visiting Maddy, Dr. Tim called to give me the good news. He did not know what caused Powder to lose her hair, but **Powder Puff did not have Cushing's disease.**

The shipper called and we decided on the exact date for my furniture to arrive at my new house. I left the warmth of Hilton Head Island for the cold of North Carolina. I am tired of driving and Powder Puff has become a horrible rider. After the trip from Canada to the United States (aka the trip to hell) she doesn't even like short trips.

Robin, Ellen, Ginger and Slick came to help me unpack the kitchen mess and small things. The movers unpacked all the furniture and placed it in the appropriate rooms. Ginger spent the night and helped with some more things in the morning. I just walked around with "my thumb up my butt." After Ginger left, I went into overdrive and completed the rest of the house. I have always worked better under pressure.

I have been living back in the states for a year. Powder Puff's hair has almost grown back. Everyone has stopped asking me, "Aren't you glad to be back in the states?" They know my answer is always the same, "Hell no, but Powder is happy."

Currently, my new mission is to help my aunt with some serious problems, which have happened to her during my absence. Many of my friends have made the comment, "Will this be another book?"

That decision is left up to you, my readers.

Epilogue

It is hard for me to believe that I have finished something that I found so enjoyable to do. This is quite an accomplishment for me, who has always been so lazy.

I am asked on a regular basis "Did you do everything you wanted to do and go everywhere you wanted to go?" Fortunately, I can answer in a positive way, although my life is not over yet. My parents afforded me the luxury and opportunity of many years to "find myself."

When I was young I hunted for sport and food on a regular basis. About twenty-five years ago, I sighted a 10-point buck, looked into his eyes, realized I was about to murder a guiltless animal, lowered my rifle and walked away. I have never picked up a gun again except for target practice. This incident led me to become a vegan, but as I got older being a vegetarian has suited me better.

I see my good friends Robin and Chuck, Chandelier, Dean and his family, Jason and his family, Martha, Maddy and Bob, Molly and Stumpie, Patsy, Marie, Wills and Susan, Toby, Ginger and Slick, and Terry and Jerry on a regular basis. Even though Liz and "DD" are both gone, I see Liz's son, Johnny and his daughter Lindsey and "DD"s daughter Missy whenever I can. I keep in touch with my out-of-state friends by phone and e-mail and with my Canadian friends the same way.

Many causes have come and gone for me, but I am now settled on the issues of Animal Rights and the continued plight of the Native Americans. I will never forget when I attempted to become a mentor for a Native American young boy and to attempt to adopt the boy. I was refused both times because of the fact that I was a young, single, Caucasian female. How times have changed!

I have lived my life on my own terms. I had the opportunity of meeting some of the most powerful people in the business world, with numerous entertainment people thrown in for good measure. My travels have been extensive and interesting.

Did I do everything I wanted to do and meet everyone I wanted to meet? Actually, I would like to complete the plans my cousin and I made years ago. I would love to meet Bob Barker. But if I don't, I will still die happy.